333.72

WAKE UP AND
SMELL THE PLANET

D0976153

WAKE UP AND SMELL THE PLANET

The Non-Pompous, Non-Preachy Grist Guide to Greening Your Day

GRIST.ORG

EDITED BY BRANGIEN DAVIS WITH KATHARINE WROTH

SKIPSTONE

ISBN 978-1-59485-039-4

Published by Skipstone, an imprint of The Mountaineers Books
Printed in Canada
First printing 2007
10 09 08 07   5 4 3 2 1

Copy Editor: Susan Hodges
Design: Heidi Smets
Cover photograph: Getty Images, Debra McClinton

Library of Congress Cataloging-in-Publication Data
Wake up and smell the planet : the nonpompous, nonpreachy grist guide to greening your day / edited by Brangien Davis and Katharine Wroth.–
1st ed.
        p. cm.
    Includes index.
    ISBN 978-1-59485-039-4 (pb)
    1. Environmentalism–United States–Popular works. 2. Sustainable living–United States—Popular works. 3. Human ecology—United States—Popular works. 4. Nature–Effect of human beings on–United States–Popular works.
I. Davis, Brangien. II. Wroth, Katharine.
GE197.W348 2007
    333.72–dc22

2007024091

Skipstone books may be purchased for corporate, educational, or other promotional sales. For special discounts and information, contact our sales department at 1-800-553-4453 or mbooks@mountaineersbooks.org.

Printed on 100% recycled paper with soy inks

Skipstone
1001 SW Klickitat Way
Suite 201
Seattle, Washington 98134
206.223.6303
www.skipstonepress.org
www.mountaineersbooks.org

Live Life. Make Ripples.

To our parents, for contributing to overpopulation, and to the
universe of Grist readers, without whom we'd be ... well, unread.

CONTENTS

WHAT A DIFFERENCE YOUR DAY MAKES

Curious about how to green your life? We figure you must be, or you wouldn't have picked up this book. (Unless you just spotted your ex browsing the next aisle. In which case, you'll want to hold it up a little higher. Because your eyebrows totally give you away.)

We also figure you might not be sure whether you have the time or energy for all this greenifying. After all, there's enough to do every day—get up, get the kids to school, go to work, take care of the dog, run errands, cook supper, tidy up, pay bills—without worrying about whether you're hurting the planet along the way. Never mind finding time to go to rallies or write letters to politicians or climb up on the roof to install solar panels. And even if you did have the time, how would you know which were the most important changes to make, or whether you were really making a difference?

Relax. That's where we come in.

Who are we, you ask? We're Grist, the green news and humor site your mother never even thought to warn you about. And we've put together a different kind of green-living book. It's a guide to making it through the day with your values—and your sanity—intact. And it's proof that you can help the planet and have a little fun along the way.

That's right: fun.

For eight years we've shown our readers—and they've shown us—that there's always a lighter side to environmental issues and quandaries. And that's what

you'll find in this book: solid advice littered with a few unexpected laughs. It's the only time we ever allow ourselves to litter, so we're pretty excited.

What else makes this book different from all the other green-living books out there? For one thing, the cover is orange. Like how we did that? It can also be used as a flotation device. More to the point, all of the ideas in these pages stem from questions our readers have asked over the years. They're people like you, people who just want to know how to make it through the day with a little less worry. People who want to protect the health of their families and of the planet.

So read on, and then come visit us any hour of the day or night at Grist.org! We'd say we'll leave the light on for you, but everyone knows that's wasteful.

—The Editors of Grist

OH, WHAT A
BEAUTIFUL
MORNING!

We bet we can guess what your morning routine looks like: You gently click off your solar-powered alarm clock, crawl out of your hemp sheets, don organic cotton slippers and a recycled fleece robe, and shuffle across your bamboo floors to the bathroom, where you bathe in rainwater and botanicals harvested from your own garden.

Not quite? Good.

Our mornings look a little different too, and we're here to praise reality. No one expects you to live a life of environmental perfection. It's hard enough to just get out of bed. But if you find yourself questioning the greenness of your routine, a few changes can help lighten your impact ... and maybe even assuage some of that guilt hanging over your bedhead.

YOU'RE SOAKING IN IT

 Most people consider bathing a fairly crucial part of the daily routine. But for those who worry about global water resources gurgling down the drain, the mere prospect of washing up can be a downer. Very few bathers have the time, space, or stamina to limit water usage to barrel-collected rainwater heated in solar sacks. Which means many of you are left standing on the bathmat, shivering in your skivvies, wondering which wastes less water—a shower or a bath?

The answer will vary depending on how long your showers are, how many gallons rain down from your showerhead each minute, how big your bathtub is, and how high you fill it when you soak. But tuck this into your robe pocket: a five-minute shower uses about a third as much water as a full bath. Whichever route you choose, there are simple things you can do to ensure your bathing experience is as water-friendly as a sea turtle:

› Fix any leaks around the faucet or showerhead (even small trickles add up to gallons of water wasted per week).

› Buy aerators for all of your faucets. These are mesh faucet ends that can cut the gallons-per-minute water usage by up to 40%. (They are easy to attach, but they may need occasional rinsing when clogged.)

› Get a low-flow showerhead, easily installable by even a tepidly intrepid person. You'll cut your water usage from about 5 gallons a minute to 2.5 gallons a minute.

> If you want to feel squeaky clean of conscience, collect the cold water that runs while your bath or shower is approaching a toasty temperature and use it to quench your plants' thirst.

> Finally, make sure you have an efficient water heater that's in working order, since warming your water accounts for 17% of home energy use. Electric heaters are generally more efficient than gas, but electricity production wastes more energy. If you're really gung ho on finding an alternative, consider a tankless heater, solar heater, on-demand heater, or a heater hooked up to the furnace in a symbiotic relationship.

Save Water, Douse an Alien

If nothing else convinces you of the importance of water conservation, consider this: Hollywood has proven that aliens, mutants, and other evil-doers are notoriously vulnerable in the face of water. Plain old water! (Okay, sometimes it's holy water or seawater, but you get the point.) Check out these movies where water saves the day:

> Signs (2002) Mel Gibson defeats aliens with H2O
> Alien Nation (1988) Salt water sizzles spotty-headed aliens
> The Lost Boys (1987) Teen vampires bitten by holy water
> The Day of the Triffids (1962) Alien plants are no match for water straight from the hose
> The Wizard of Oz (1939) Two words: "I'm melting!"

The moral? Save water: You never know when you might need it.

NO VINYL. THAT'S FINAL.

One way to improve your bathing experience immediately is to get rid of your vinyl shower curtain. In fact, vinyl creeps into a lot of facets of life, so it's good to get it out of the way first thing in the morning.

PVC, or polyvinyl chloride, is the fancy name for vinyl, a type of plastic. The vinyl we're familiar with was invented in the 1920s by a man with the delightful name of Waldo Semon. There are other types of vinyl, with acronyms like PVA and PVB, but PVC is the most common, and it is what people are generally referring to when they use the word *vinyl*.

Altruism-attempting eco-heads must enforce a personal shopping ban on all PVC and vinyl products. Polyvinyl chloride creates dioxins during manufacture, use, and disposal. Dioxin is a known carcinogen that can also disrupt hormonal systems and may cause reproductive and immune system damage.

So don't bring any #3 plastic, vinyl, or PVC into your life, including the part where you are naked and trying to keep water from spilling all over the bathroom floor. Rip down that shower curtain or hack it to shreds in the style of Norman Bates, whatever you please, but get rid of it and don't ever buy another.

SOME 63% OF AMERICANS SHOWER ONCE OR MORE A DAY.

Seek out a cotton or polyester replacement. Neither is a perfect option; cotton farming requires ridiculous amounts of pesticides and polyester is another type of plastic (albeit less harmful), so petroleum, noxious chemicals, and massive processing are common to both. Alternatively, you could look for an organic cotton or hemp liner, or make your own from worn-out clothing. (Just think, a whole new use for your collection of Bon Jovi "Slippery When Wet" T-shirts!) But since few people will spend the money or time to do that, cotton and polyester win this "which is better?" dilemma.

HIRSUTE YOURSELF

While we're on the topic of morning rituals, we must address a certain hairy question. If you're trying to live a more environmentally friendly lifestyle, is shaving misbehaving?

It's true, the best option is not to shave at all. What a different world it would be if we all proceeded according to the lyrics from *Hair* ("Flow it! Show it! Long beautiful hair!"). But since life isn't a Broadway musical and workplace conventions (or those picky personal tastes) probably prohibit you from embracing your inner Sasquatch, we have some suggestions.

First and foremost, stop using disposable plastic razors. The arguments against them are many, including where the plastic comes from, how much fuel is consumed just getting them to your drugstore, and the effect on the waste stream. Here in the United States, two billion disposable razors are purchased annually. That's a lot of space in the landfill.

In addition to the environmental concern, there's, well, the dorkiness. Shaving should be sexy, and a choice opportunity to impress that special someone. Plastic disposables say, "I think little about personal grooming," not to mention "I'm cheap," and when it comes to romance there is little margin for this type of drastic plastic error.

So what's the alternative? Electric razors won't do, because they use electricity. Not much, maybe 15 watts, but if we're going to talk about the impact of shaving, we might as well split hairs. The same goes for electric shavers with rechargeable batteries, lasers, and electrolysis, all of which also produce greenhouse gases. (Not in your bathroom, of course—that's a different kind of gas—but during the production and transmission of the electricity that powers them.) As for depilatory creams, any person with a working nostril knows they are toxic.

Brave men might choose a straight razor, which would place you in the rarefied echelon of sexy enviro-men who remain low-hair with confidence, style, and danger. Also, the straight-razor purist uses only solid soap, creating another opportunity for waste reduction (viz. those aerosol cans of cream). However, people don't signify death by pantomiming a razor blade under the neck for nothing.

Brave women might go with "body sugaring," in which you concoct your own wax (a heated paste of sugar, water, and lemon juice) and slather your legs in it. After letting the sticky mixture set, you apply recycled strips of cotton fabric and, as they say, let 'er rip. But if you find the phrase "just like a Band-Aid" less than comforting, you may want to reconsider.

A permanent razor that uses refillable blades is a reasonable option for both men and women; granted, the handle is plastic, but you can use it repeatedly and thereby reduce both your guilt and your garbage. You might also seek out razors made of recycled plastic. Recycline's "Preserve" brand uses 100% recycled materials (mainly yogurt cups) and can be found online, in environmentally conscious grocery stores, and even at Target.

Abolish Polish

If you are willing to give up just one beauty product, make it nail polish. A 2006 study by the National Asian Pacific American Women's Forum reported that the nail industry uses 10,000 chemicals in its products, 89% of which have not been safety tested by any independent agency, and some of which are known or suspected carcinogens. There is no purely nontoxic nail polish, although some brands claim the title by reducing chemical compounds and fragrances. Trouble is, you have to get that stuff off your nails somehow, and we all know that noxious, flammable, eye-irritating acetone is the most effective method. If you can't bear to leave your nails bare, at least paint them less frequently and in a well ventilated room—and stay away from the fume fiesta of the nail salon.

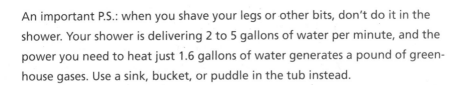

An important P.S.: when you shave your legs or other bits, don't do it in the shower. Your shower is delivering 2 to 5 gallons of water per minute, and the power you need to heat just 1.6 gallons of water generates a pound of greenhouse gases. Use a sink, bucket, or puddle in the tub instead.

COSMETICS: A LESS-THAN-ROSY VIEW

All toweled off and feeling fresh? Good, because it's time to talk about greening your makeup. No, that doesn't mean resurrecting the emerald eye shadow

Natural skin care and beauty products no longer translate to straw hair and a blemished face. In fact, the industry has taken great strides in creating products that glow, shimmer, and shine, while paying close attention to both global sustainability and personal health. Consider these face- and earth-friendly cosmetic brands, increasingly available in major grocery stores, at many drugstores, and online:

> Aubrey Organics (*www.aubrey-organics.com*)
> Avalon Organics (*www.avalonorganics.com*)
> Aveda (*www.aveda.com*)
> Badger Balm (*www.badgerbalm.com*)
> Burt's Bees (*www.burtsbees.com*)
> Ecco Bella (*www.eccobella.com*)
> Jason Natural Cosmetics (*www.jason-natural.com*)
> Kiss My Face (*www.kissmyface.com*)
> Zia Naturals (*www.zianatural.com*)

Shimmers of Hope in the Beauty Palette

But if you're a stalwart brand loyalist, keep in mind:

> Refills are par for the course with eye shadow;
> MAC cosmetics accepts old makeup containers with a return-six-and-get-one-lipstick-free policy;
> Pencil eyeliners can be used down to the nub—and mascara ... well, it seems like it could just be refilled at the local tar shop.

your mother used to favor (though she did look fetching). It means opting out of the "beauty" industry as much as you can …. Because you're worth it!

As anyone who's torn through layers of plastic and cardboard to get to a compact knows, unnecessary packaging comes with the cosmetic territory. In addition to the wrapping gone overboard, consider what happens when you decide it's time to ditch Blushing Berry for Pouty Pink. Discarded cosmetics and other personal-care products (deodorant, toothpaste, etc.) are either consumed by burning, burning incinerator love or shmooshed in the landfill sandwich. The sundry ingredients, when reduced to ash or ooze, may escape into the surrounding air, land, and water and attack the natural world with their potentially noxious properties (see below). The likelihood of escape depends on the security of the incinerator or landfill. Notice how we went from packaging to disposal? We skipped the part where you slather yourself with chemicals. Every. Single. Day.

Many personal-care products contain ingredients whose health effects are untested or, worse, ingredients *known* to pose health risks, according to a report from the Environmental Working Group and other nonprofits. Only a small percentage of the chemical ingredients used in such products in the United States have been tested for safety, and those tests were overseen by industry-related review boards. Most individual ingredients don't pose worrisome risks, but because people use many different products—an average of ten per day for U.S. adults—risks could add up.

Less harmful cosmetics contain fewer solvents (the chemicals that keep substances liquid or help them dry quickly) and volatile organic compounds (which go into the flowery fragrances we're so fond of) and will tout said accomplishment on the packaging. As for buying "natural" cosmetics, just be sure you read the fine print. While splashy terms and phrases such as "earth-friendly," "organic," "nontoxic," and "no harmful fragrances" can occasionally be helpful, the ugly truth is in the ingredient list. To find out more about the ingredients in your favorite products, as well as the companies that are turning things around, visit the Campaign for Safe Cosmetics (*www.safecosmetics.org*).

The bottom line: although their purported function is to improve your social environment, cosmetics are bad for your personal environment, and for the waste stream when you're done with them. Cut down on these toxics and you'll do everyone a favor. You'll still look good—and you might just feel good too.

THE BREAKFAST OF CHAMPIONS

As you've probably figured out, attempting to embrace a more "eco" lifestyle can require keeping your mind on hyperalert. What to others might look like a routine day could start feeling like a rapid-fire barrage of the same question, over and over: *What would the earth want me to do?* Coffee can be a very good friend in these wakeful moments, offering tasty cupfuls of fortitude for split-second decision making. But, alas, like many mood-altering drugs, it comes with a few strings attached.

LABEL CONSCIOUS

When it comes to coffee, shade-grown, fair-trade, and organic aren't just buzz-words. All three are certifications that resulted from a desire to ensure that our caffeine addictions support sustainable agriculture and fair labor standards, rather than reinforcing the system of displaced workers toiling in serfdom on devastated land. Coffee that meets all three standards is called "triple certified." You can determine legitimacy by doing a little easy sleuthing: check for labels or ask your barista.

FAIR TRADE

This certification indicates that producers and workers receive a fair price for their goods, and the production process considers social, economic, and environmental factors. It requires annual inspections, fees, and filings. At present, Fair Trade certification is controlled by Fairtrade Labelling Organizations International, and its U.S. arm, TransFair USA, pastes a standard label on certified products. There are some concerns about the fair-trade movement inflating prices and imposing unwieldy rules on producers, but in general it is an excellent hope for sustainable development worldwide and is worth supporting.

ORGANIC

This certification uses a process similar to fair-trade but focuses on food production methods, not price or labor specifications. The International Federation of Organic Agriculture Movements provides an umbrella organization and voluntary agreement on organic basics. In the United States, the U.S. Department of

Agriculture certifies producers and processors, as do some private and state entities. There is a standard label in this case, too, and no end of squabbling about its meaningfulness. But the label is usually a better bet than an "organic" brand that isn't certified.

SHADE-GROWN

While organic and fair-trade are organized and widespread eco-labels, shade-grown certification is a bit less formalized at this point. The Smithsonian Migratory Bird Center and the Rainforest Alliance both offer third-party labels that verify the maintenance of diverse forest and bird habitat on coffee planta-tions. Currently, shade-grown is not a make-or-break certification for addicts, in part because it is the least prevalent and least specific. Sorry, birdies!

CUP OF KINDNESS

Now that you've had your coffee consciousness raised, how to best transport your morning transfusion?

The primary goal is to reduce disposable cup use by relying on longer-lived mugs. Most of us have three basic mug options: petroleum plastic, stainless steel, and ceramic. (Corn plastic is reportedly on the rise, so watch for maize mugs coming from a field near you!)

Ceramics are great if you're planning to hang out in the coffeehouse all day, but if you're on the go, your lidless latte will soon be in your lap. Portable joe

METHYLENE CHLORIDE, SOME-TIMES USED TO DECAFFEINATE COFFEE, IS ALSO A PAINT STRIPPER.

Should you want some vittles to complement your morning coffee, be sure you're awake enough to check the labels. An unhealthy sweetener called high-fructose corn syrup (HFCS) lurks in many popular breakfast options—even "healthy" ones like juice, yogurt, bread, granola bars, and cereal. Between 1975 and 1997, per-capita consumption of HFCS in the United States jumped from virtually nothing to 60.4 pounds per year—equal to about 200 calories per person, per day—and it's hovered around that level since. For manufacturers, it's a cheap source of calories and flavor, but all this convenience comes with a price: HFCS has been linked to obesity and type 2 diabetes. Now is that any way to treat the most important meal of the day?

requires plastic or steel, and working backward from the reducing-disposables goal, plastics appear to be shorter-lived than stainless. They become scratched and kind of pilly, start to smell odd, until finally one day, justly dubious of their cleanliness and certain of their scruffiness, we dump them. Stainless, on the other hand, will hold its sleek look over time.

In addition, stainless steel is a fairly decent, durable material. Large volumes of stainless steel are reclaimed and reprocessed; globally, stainless steel contains

Twenty-two-year-old fashion model Summer Rayne Oakes has a fondness for bugs. A Cornell University graduate with a background in natural resources and entomology, she's more than a pretty face. Oakes models only clothing made from organic or recycled materials, and says the $400 billion global textile industry's reliance on pesticides, herbicides, and toxic dyes is a significant, underreported problem. She also cites the 40 million people employed in clothing trades, many working for a pittance. While eco-activists seldom mention it, Oakes believes that fashion "offers exceptionally good opportunities to talk about ecological issues, as well as fair trade and labor standards."

Standing tall at 5 feet, 11 inches, the self-described "eco-style expert" explains the challenges of constructing slinky undergarments from organic cotton—the fibers wear out too quickly, especially when compared to the conventionally produced equivalent. But she predicts a bright future for sustainable lace, and fabric production in general. One of the reasons, Oakes says, is that "we can do amazing things with chemistry."

These days, she's taking her message wider as a TV host and consultant. And wherever she goes, Oakes steers clear of the stereotypical eco-garb of hemp ponchos or sack dresses. Donning tight, trendy digs "can rope viewers or readers in," she admits. "But I always make sure that the substance and message aren't far behind."

an average of 60% recycled content. Unfortunately, virgin stainless, which may well be in travel mugs, is very high in "embodied energy," meaning its manufacture uses many resources and is likely worse than the manufacture of plastics (corn or petroleum). But duration of end-use can make up for the embodied energy costs, i.e., a stainless cup used daily for five years probably beats a plastic cup used for six months. And either one is better than a paper cup used for sixty minutes.

CLOTHES ENCOUNTERS

For some, it's the toughest decision to make in the morning: *what to wear, what to wear?* And it only gets tougher when you start thinking about the chemicals used in processing fabric, developing-world textile workers slaving under inhumane conditions, and the mass consumerism promoted by the clothing industry. In fact, it's tempting to go naked. Before you decide to go public with your privates, however, educate yourself and consider the alternatives.

DREAD OF THREADS

You'll be hard-pressed to find a common textile that isn't soberingly toxic to produce. It makes sense if you think about the raw materials—wood, cotton, oil, sheep, cows—and what it might involve to transform them into a nice outfit.

All textiles, as currently manufactured, require large volumes of water throughout the manufacturing process. Spinning, dyeing, weaving, scouring, sizing—all involve flushing the threads or fabric with water at one point or another, and often that water comes away contaminated with chemicals used earlier in the process, including dioxin-producing bleach.

Hemp: Not Just for Hippies

Hemp is currently a narrowly available (notably nonsmokable) fabric with a prohibitively high cost and a limited fashion palette. That said, it holds a lot of promise as a high-yield crop with a boggling array of uses, including rope, carpets, shoes, cars, food, fuel, and oil, that suggest it could one day save the world.

China, Eastern Europe, and Canada are the big hemp-producing regions. In the United States, the world-changing capacity of hemp is absurdly curtailed because of knee-jerk drug laws: Hemp is outlawed along with the similar, but not identical, marijuana plant. Hemp research plots are under cultivation in several states, but the federal government still prohibits commercial plantings.

Part of the high cost of hemp textiles can be blamed on low availability; it also stems from the unsuitability of hemp fibers for machines designed to process cotton, polyester, and wood. Of course, the length and toughness of its fibers also means hemp can be grown with very few pesticides and herbicides, partly because the plant creates too much shade for weeds to thrive. (Not that hemp is perfect: The conversion of hemp fiber to fabric, like many textile processes, generally involves the use of water and bleach.)

Should you have the money and inclination to buy and wear hemp, go ahead. Just don't blame it for your munchies.

So, while no garment is perfect, and we know it's what's on the inside that counts, here's a rundown of the pros and cons in your closet.

Cotton is renewable, but it is not grown sustainably. The Pesticide Action Network says that cotton production accounts for 10% of world pesticide use, and nearly 25% of world insecticide use. Pesticides are used not only to deter pests, but also to defoliate plants for harvesting convenience.

Synthetic/cotton blends are usually treated with formaldehyde (which may account for the continued sightings of a well-preserved Elvis).

Rayon is made from cellulose (wood pulp, with its own relationship to poor forestry practices), and talk about toxic: As it turns out, sulfuric acid comes in handy when transforming a tree into a chemise. Fabrication of petroleum-based fabrics like **nylon** and **polyester** is energy-intensive and greenhouse-gas producing. And **wool**? Well, sheep are often bathed in organophosphates to control parasites.

If you're hell-bent for **leather**, this may chap your hide: Tanning is the process of turning part of a formerly living animal into a nonrotting, soft, durable textile. Hair and flesh are removed, edges are trimmed, and the remaining skin is cured, stretched, and dried. Some steps in the process can be achieved physically, while others are achieved chemically. The process creates wastewater that can include chemicals and "solids" (i.e., useless parts of the ex-animal suspended in water), which put a strain on water-treatment systems and, if left undisturbed, can harm aquatic life forms. Also, oils and grease from the animal fat can clog treatment systems and generally gum up everything in sight.

But wait, there's more!

Many of the chemicals used to produce and process fabrics, dye them, make them wrinkle-free, clean them, and keep them from becoming insect nests during shipping will give off gas. According to the "experts," it's rare for the body to absorb chemicals directly from clothes. That means the people who bear the brunt of toxins in apparel are laborers in other countries, where workplace safety and water-quality protections are sub-standard, to put it nicely.

In short, the clothing industry is full of dirty laundry.

TIPS FOR TOGS

If you're concerned about your wardrobe, there are several things you can do. First, think about buying more natural fibers like wool, hemp, and cotton. You will find a bounty of organic and sustainable clothing companies if you spend time poking around on the Internet. But even industrially produced natural-fiber clothes share admirable aspects with their sustainable cousins. They don't generate much static electricity in the dryer (eliminating the need for those toxic dryer sheets), they generally require less (or no) toxic dry cleaning, they're made from renewable resources, and after you're done with them, they can be composted. Try doing that with your polyester leisure suit! (Actually, please don't.)

RECYCLED DENIM CAN BE USED AS A GREEN REPLACEMENT FOR FIBERGLASS INSULATION

You could also go the crafty route and make your own clothes. But the reality is that most of us don't have the time (or skills) for hours spent hunched over a sewing machine. So here's another trick: buy from secondhand shops. This

Clothes that Care

When you really do need something new, turn to companies that are attempting to make a dent in the damage the textile industry is doing. Big retailers like the Gap, Levi's, and Patagonia have begun to embrace organic cotton. Here are a few more trendsetters.

> **Clothes:** American Apparel, cool not cruel, Del Forte Denim, Earth Bitch, Loomstate, Rawganique, Romp, Shirts of Bamboo
> **Shoes:** Black Spot, Charmone, Simple, Terra Plana

way you'll not only adhere to the second R in the recycling triad (reduce! reuse! recycle!), but you'll also give the clothes time to offgas the various toxins they were birthed or bathed in during manufacture. To the uninitiated it may seem that used clothes are dowdy, ripped, worn out, and available only in unattractive stores. To the addicted, however, secondhand clothing stores are a treasure trove of budget-friendly fashion. Buying used clothing for your kids is an especially good plan for both their health and your wallet, since wee ones have a tendency to grow out of their wee clothing quickly.

Finally, if you stick with buying new synthetic fabrics, know that they generally get less off-gassy with time, due to the effects of age, wear, and multiple washings.

Whatever kind of clothing you buy, make sure to wash all new-to-you duds with natural laundry soap at least once before wearing. This will help excise any residues from manufacturing or from previous washings in chemical-ridden mainstream detergents.

WHERE DO CLOTHES GO WHEN THEY DIE?

So it's finally time to bid adieu to those holey socks—should you chuck 'em? In our modern, throwaway society, most people assume that when rags die, they're buried in a landfill. But there actually are domestic and foreign markets for our discards.

Those of us who have gotten over our old get-ups can reach these markets through donation sites that—on the surface—appear to take only usable clothing. Goodwill, for instance, bales unusable clothing and sends it for recycling and reuse, which helps support its programs. Similar organizations in your area may also do this. (A phone query is recommended before assuming your discards will be welcome, as some local businesses may be too small to broker them.)

Your discards will be reused by people in faraway countries, shredded to fill car seats, used as industrial-type wipes, or reworked into textiles. Special note to word hounds: shredded, used textile material that's ready to be integrated into a new item is called *shoddy*.

Should you want to take care of your own shoddy business, you might consider repurposing your old natural fabrics in the garden, either composting them or using them for mulch as one would use a burlap sack. Another idea is to call around to animal shelters to see if they can use your large rags for bedding or cleanup.

And you thought they were just holey socks.

OH, BABY!

Getting out the door in the morning can be stressful enough, but those of you who have chosen to spawn have complicated matters even further. (What are you, masochists?) Generally, you can apply the same environmental principles about bathing, clothing, and consuming to your children's lives that you would to your own life. But there is one special case we must address specifically: the case of the adorably cheeked consumption machine, your baby.

NURSERY RHYME AND REASON

Babies. So cutesy-wutesy, itty-bitty, eensy-weensy—and kinda helpless, really. Which means there are at least two things they're no good at: bowling, and coping with toxic substances. Chemicals that have a mild effect on most adults can have a stronger impact on the smaller bodies and unpracticed immune systems of young humans. It can be hard to toe the line between reasonable caution and massive freak-outs when it comes to one's children, but the aim is to do the best you can. One good way to limit your wee one's exposure to environmental hazards is to start with the nursery.

When it comes to setting up your bundle of joy's digs, you can accomplish twin goals: reducing consumption and reducing toxics. The first strategy to keep in mind is buying only what you need. Talk with experienced parents or professionals about the equipment that is necessary and useful, and be clear with your gift-giving family and friends that you welcome most used goods, but want only certain new goods. Don't fret that you will offend people—after all, what's better than knowing a gift is useful?

Try to be imaginative as well as minimalist with baby room equipment. Your baby doesn't care whether you buy a cutting-edge changing table or plop a changing pad on top of an old dresser. Certain pieces can do double duty and your existing furniture or local consignment store may do just fine.

As you go about finding whatever new goods you buy, follow a few guidelines:

On the Eco-Parent's Bookshelf

There are many relevant books out there; here are a few to get you started:

> *Green Parenting,* by Melissa Corkhill
> *The Complete Organic Pregnancy,* by Deirdre Dolan and Alexandra Zissu
> *A Mother's Guide to Raising Healthy Children—Naturally,* by Sue Frederick
> *Raising Healthy Children in a Toxic World,* by Philip J. Landrigan, Herbert L. Needleman, and Mary M. Landrigan
> *Natural Family Living,* by Peggy O'Mara
> *The Natural Nursery: The Parent's Guide to Ecologically Sound, Nontoxic, Safe, and Healthy Baby Care* by Louis Pottkotter, MD

- Use milk-based or other natural paints that don't contain volatile organic compounds (VOCs).

- Install a wood or linoleum floor, not carpeting. Synthetic carpeting can give off noxious fumes, and also tends to attract dust mites, mold, and mildew.

- Whether the furniture is new or old, invest in well-built pieces instead of going with plywood or pressed wood, which can contain formaldehyde.

- Be sure your house and furniture are free of lead paint.

- Don't buy products labeled "known to the state of California to cause cancer or reproductive toxicity." (Duh.)

Putting a little thought behind your baby's boudoir should let you rest easy. Unfortunately we can make no such promises about the kid.

ARE ALL DIAPERS DIABOLICAL?

Any new parent knows having a baby means dealing with a ton of dirty diapers. But fewer realize that the average baby produces literally *one ton* of soiled diapers before potty training kicks in. So what's the best way to deal with that doo-doo that kids do so well?

THE NATIONAL ACTIVIST GROUP MAKING OUR MILK SAFE (MOMS) FORMED AFTER A ROCKET-FUEL COMPONENT WAS FOUND IN BREAST MILK.

Many eco-parents embrace cloth diapers, based on their reusability and a lesser likelihood of exposing sensitive baby skin to dyes and absorbent gels. Perhaps the strongest argument for cloth diapers is that they won't end up festering forever in landfills. But many

A company in the Pacific Northwest has recently attempted to make peace among the warring diaper diehards with a product called GDiapers (*www.gdiapers.com*), which offer yet a third option: a chlorine-free, dye-free, perfume-free flushable diaper, which combines the convenience of a disposable with the happy feeling one gets when not contributing to landfills. The washable outer layer is made from 100% biodegradable natural fibers and the flushable inner layer is composed of compostable natural fibers, plus tree-farmed fluff pulp for absorbency.

others claim that disposable is the way to go, since the cleaning process for cloth diapers—whether you use a service or do it yourself—uses too much water (to wash) and energy (to dry) to be considered sustainable. In addition, the plastic covers required to prevent wetness are usually made with PVCs. Folks on the disposable side of the great diaper debate also point out that there are now many options on the market that aren't produced with the dyes and plastics used by the mega-brands.

Examples in this new wave of earth-friendlier varieties include Seventh Generation, TenderCare, and Nature Boy & Girl brands, which are reputedly chlorine-free and replace plastic ingredients with wood pulp and cornstarch.

In the grand scheme of things, the debate over the relative merits of cloth versus disposable diapers, like the one over paper versus plastic bags, tends to arouse passions out of proportion to its significance. In 2005, the U.K. Environment Agency attempted to settle the question once and for all. It released the results of a four-year study that analyzed three diaper types—disposable, home-washed cloth, and professionally washed cloth—from manufacture to disposal. The verdict? It doesn't matter.

No Rest for Nappies

Some 20 billion diapers are buried in U.S. landfills per year, representing about 7 billion pounds of garbage. In 2002, Santa Clarita, California, a suburb of Los Angeles, was the first municipality in the United States to institute a diaper-recycling program, planning to transform the soiled, disposable sacks of goodies into oil filters, roof shingles, and vinyl siding. But after a trial period of nine months (hmm), the city council called it quits, saying the $500,000 program cost too much. The company Santa Clarita worked with, called Knowaste, can recycle up to 98% of a diaper into reusable wood pulp and plastic pellets and runs diaper-recycling facilities in Canada, Australia, and the Netherlands. So at least diapers are doing double duty in those parts of the world!

No, really, it doesn't. Both manufacturers and parents could do more to reduce their ecological impact, but the choice between cloth and disposable is one of personal preference. Said Tracey Stewart of the Absorbent Hygiene Products Manufacturers' Association (who knew!), "No one anymore can claim the moral high ground on nappies."

GOING COMMANDO

And finally: In a seemingly radical departure from the entire diaper dilemma, some folks have decided to pooh-pooh the question altogether and go without. People around the world who have no access to diapers still manage to raise children, and some parents in diaper-rich countries are following their lead. It's called "elimination communication" or "diaper-free." The concept is logical and simple: Infants give recognizable signs of imminent peeing and pooping; it's possible to learn your infant's signs; infant pee isn't frightening; and if you train your kids to ignore their outputs, you'll just have to go back and retrain them when potty-training time arrives.

So what kind of parents would be likeliest to succeed with this mind-blowingly logical technique? Parents and caregivers need to be able to pay close attention to the child and be comfortable being unusual. If you think you might fit the bill, there are gobs of resources on the web for this retro, cutting-edge scheme. Check out *www.Natural-Wisdom.com* for starters. Be the first in your neighborhood!

A Green Guide for Your Mini-Me

Those of you who spend great scads of the morning getting young-sters out the door have plenty on your plate. So we'll make it easy (easier?) for you, with a quick checklist for making sure the kids are all right:

> A healthy breakfast, with nary a drop of high-fructose corn syrup.
> An outfit consisting of gently used hand-me-downs, cool Goodwill finds, or organic, pesticide-free, and sweatshop-shunning threads.
> A vinyl-free backpack (look for hemp or recycled rubber models), packed with vinyl-free binders and chlorine-free recycled paper.
> A cloth lunch sack holding locally grown, organic foods wrapped in waxed paper.
> A family bonding (and exercise inducing!) walk or bike to school with parents, friends, or neighbors—or, second-best, a carpool.
> A totally sustainable, always renewable kiss and hug.

PET PROJECTS

As any pet owner knows, no morning would be complete without attending to the gastrointestinal needs of our furry friends. Among the multitude of unsavory chores we endure in the name of our beloved animal companions, disposing of feces is surely the most disgusting. Perhaps we can make it somewhat less offensive by offering a few tips for making those excretions more eco? Eh, probably not, but they're still handy.

PICK OF THE LITTER

Cats are pretty discreet about dealing with their own doo-doo, but they aren't so skilled at emptying the litter box. There are a couple options for avoiding the tyranny of the box altogether, but both have drawbacks. The first is to let your cat go outside, but that isn't an option for many urban dwellers, and there's a vocal contingent of animal lovers who will enumerate the dangers of letting Fluffy out (first and foremost, cars and the associated squish potential). The second, wackier choice might be to train your cat to use the toilet, which has proven miraculous in many cases (Google and learn). The problem with this

decision, besides the possible tails of woe, is that more and more evidence has shown that cat feces should never enter our sewage systems.

The issue is a parasite called *Toxoplasmosis Gondii* (TG), which many (but not all) domestic cats carry. This little bugger is the reason experts warn pregnant women never to handle cat feces. While it doesn't appear to affect other members of the family or pets, it does harm water quality and marine life; apparently, TG is resistant to standard sewage treatment measures, and slips through the process unzapped. It is now believed that nearly 20% of all sea lion deaths can be blamed on TG. Accordingly, California (home of many sea lions) has made it illegal to dispose of cat feces in the sewer systems. So even if your kitty litter claims to be "flushable," it's a better choice to bag it and throw it in the garbage, especially if you live in a coastal area. If you do, look forward to a flippered salute.

For the Discerning Eco-Feline

When it comes to the scoop on litter, today's cat owner has a wide choice of options, including products made from recycled paper, wood, corn, and even green tea leaves. "Swheat Scoop," for example, is made from naturally processed wheat, and is clay-free, fragrance-free, chemical-free, and biodegradable. "Feline Pine" consists of 100% natural, biodegradable pine pellets that have been heated and pressurized to remove harmful wood oils. It also boasts that its clumping power comes from Guar beans (so it's practically a salad!). You might also consider adding baking soda to the box, which can keep things fresher longer, requiring less litter in the long run.

An alternative for the truly motivated (and nonpregnant) is to compost your catbox contents. You should use a separate container from your other compost, but it doesn't need to be fancy—a small trash can with holes in the bottom and a tight lid will be fine. Just put the soiled litter in, and after the poop has been anaerobically composting for over a year, spread it on your ornamental plants—but *not* in your vegetable garden. Or you can bury fresh feces in a foot-deep hole, though not within 100 feet of a water source. If you have kids playing in your yard, it's probably best to stick with the trash.

A final note to anyone going the traditional litter box route (and then we promise to stop talking about cat poop): please eschew "clumping" brands that use clay. Bentonite clay is a nonbiodegradable substance that is strip-mined to make cat litter, which is not only destructive to the natural environment, but ridiculous. We strip mine just so our cats' urine will clump? In addition, these litters give off dust clouds containing silica, a known carcinogen.

PICKING UP WHERE FIDO LEAVES OFF

Dog owners are accustomed to coming in contact with nasty substances, and one of the nastiest is—you guessed it—plastic. Responsible dog lovers are beholden to plastic bags, since paper and poop are not a good combo and leaving land mines for unsuspecting outdoors enthusiasts doesn't go over well, either. But if purchasing new plastic for your pooch has you, er, down in the dumps, read on.

63% OF AMERICAN HOUSE-HOLDS OWN A PET (BUT DO THEY SHOWER WITH THEM?)

Old Dog Poop, New Tricks

Renewable energy is the shit. No, really. San Francisco Bay Area cities are aiming to generate no trash by 2020, and nearly 4% of San Francisco's residential waste is animal excrement. What to do with the doo? Turn it into methane and heat your home or cook your meals with it! (Your reaction to this idea is perhaps a good test of exactly how far you want to go with this whole living green thing.) In 2006, a San Francisco sanitation company began collecting feces at busy dog parks and sending it to be digested by hungry bacteria. The resulting methane could theoretically be used in any natural-gas system; some officials hope to see methane digesters in individual homes within a few years. While it's a relatively newfangled notion in the United States, some European countries already process poo into energy. If San Francisco is any indication, dog owners are happy to have someone else handle the goods. Reports a company spokesman: "[Locals] have offered all kinds of 'help' to get the program off the ground."

The simplest solution is to find pals or coworkers with stockpiles of plastic sacks and become the local bag reuse center. While trolling for bag collectors, you can spread the anti-plastic-sack doctrine, as well as assist those people afflicted with a constant source of plastic bags: newspaper subscribers. You certainly know at least one person who receives his or her newspaper wrapped in a plastic bag every day and would undoubtedly welcome your overtures.

Another option: biodegradable, flushable dog-poop bags. The general idea is that you take pup out for a stroll, pick up the poop, and then carry the filled bag back home to the toilet bowl. Of course, on long walks, the designated poop scooper usually can't find a trash can soon enough. Carrying the stuff all the way home sounds vile, but if these bags head for the landfill, their degradability will be wasted; they need to be submerged in water to dissolve.

It's hard to know which to recommend, given the cost of buying bags specifically for dog poop and the revulsion factor of carrying excrement around town on the one hand, and, on the other, the fact that regular plastic bags degrade on a geologic timescale and gum up the works in landfills.

If you are so inclined, you could try composting your dog doo. The good old Internet offers a wide array of strategies, all of which involve digging a deep hole in your yard (far away from any water source), adding "digester" or "septic starter" to encourage bacteria growth, and leaving it all covered for a long, long time. The waste will eventually biodegrade into the subsoil, and should not, we repeat, *not* be collected and used as fertilizer for your garden.

Even if you choose to use this method, when you walk your dog beyond your yard (and you should), using plastic bags is pretty unavoidable. So, uh, make up for it by taking the bus to work a couple days a week!

Morning Grist in Five Seconds or Less

The best part of waking up is:

A. Organic java in your cup
B. A long, hot shower on full blast
C. Composting your kitty litter
D. Your shoddy wardrobe

If you answered B, you're still a little sleepy. Go back to bed!

LET'S MAKE A DAY OF IT

So you're up-and-at-'em and ready to face the world. Now what? For some of us, the next step is heading to that institution where we spend half of our waking hours: Starbucks. And for the rest of us, it's time to go to work. Whether you're a pipefitter or a professor of medieval studies, you don't have to check your eco-habits at the door. We'll help you make your days—and your company—greener.

Note: If your day's work involves running errands, transporting kids here and there, or other nonoffice activities, you don't get to skip this part. You still participate in all the consumption an average day entails, and if you can incorporate even a few changes into your weekday routine, you'll be doing the environment a major favor.

COMMUTE-ICABLE DISEASES

First of all, if you can telecommute, do! Stay-at-home parents and people who work from home can create a much smaller impact on the environment, especially if you clump out-of-home errands together in one car trip (or better

Take that Pedal Off the Metal

In 1973, 55 mph was decreed the national speed limit. It was lifted in rural areas in 1987, but stuck around as federal law until 1995. Every single "Tips for Saving Gas" list still tells you to drive 55 mph, but very few tell you why.

The basic reasoning comes down to physics. Driving slower means less "drag," and thus less effort by the engine. Drag is aerodynamic resistance, basically. You've felt it if you've ever walked with a banner in a parade, or pushed against a heavy wind in a flapping coat. That's the same drag a car experiences as it pushes forward on the road—it fights the air, it fights the friction of the road, it fights the urge to pull off and get a Big Mac. And instead of burning lunch to fight drag, it burns gas. The more drag, the more gas.

So is 55 the magic number? By many estimates it's pretty darn close, though each vehicle has its own speed of maximum efficiency dependent on engines, car bodies, and driving conditions. Gas mileage decreases rapidly at speeds above 60; boosting your highway speed from 55 to 75 can raise fuel consumption by as much as 20%. Driving at steady, reasonable speeds will save both gas and money.

SPEED
LIMIT
55

yet, do them by bike or on foot). Leaving your car in the driveway even one or two days a week can make a big difference. Many companies are realizing the benefits of supporting telecommuting: Easing commutes reduces our stress, which makes us happier, more productive, less prone to call in sick, and likelier to stick around. All of which has a positive financial impact for employers. If you can't telecommute, live close to work. Walking or biking to work not only reduces emissions, it gets those quads burning.

If it's impossible for you to live near your job, use public transportation, car share, or carpool. Are you seeing where we're going with this? The least favorable option is to take a daily, solo drive to work.

I LIKE BIKE

Biking not only maintains but improves your health, in terms of muscles and heart rate and mental peace, and has little impact on the environment. It beats motorized vehicles of all types on both these counts. But is it safe to bike in traffic, breathing all those fumes?

Lungwise, it's at least as safe as driving, if not more so. Chemicals and particulate matter flow from car and bus and taxi engines and into the mini-weather system of the traffic zone.

Those nasties—including carbon monoxide and benzene—are densest at the middle of the traffic zone, and less intense on the edges. There are many variables for air-pollution scientists to play with, and each situation is different, but basically, studies show you get the biggest hit of the nasties when you're inside a car. Sure, a personal Mobile Emissions Source appears hermetic, but it's an illusion: MES occupants are very close to sucking on the tailpipe of the MES just ahead of them. In a bus, riders' lungs are a bit above these sources. And bikers and pedestrians, though they may be breathing more heavily than sedentary drivers, are on the outskirts.

If you intend to start a biking habit, use common sense. Evaluate your own confidence and experience. If you never see a single cyclist on the route you would take to work, find out where the decent bike route lies. Ask fellow cyclists whether they consider your route safe. Find the bike lanes, the roads with good shoulders. Every major city has a bicycling coalition, and many publish route maps. And if you're still worried about fumes, you could always wear a mask.

Dive Into Carpooling

If we're going to remain a car-obsessed nation, the least we can do is carpool. Think about this: the average U.S. commuter travels approximately 15 miles one way to get to work each day. If you share a ride with someone, that's 7,500 miles a year the second car doesn't have to go—saving about 300 gallons of gas. At today's prices, that's no small shakes.

If you agree to go this route, you can lessen the impact by taking the most efficient vehicle possible. When choosing between Patty's Prius or Hugh's Hummer, you probably know which is best. Whatever you drive, try to keep your speed to 55-ish if you safely can—that will help you save gas.

CHOOSE WISELY

The decision to purchase a car, and which car you purchase, is one of the most significant environmental choices you will ever make.

(We'll pause briefly to let that sink in.)

(Still pausing.)

Vehicles consume half the world's oil and spew a quarter of its greenhouse gas emissions. Burning a single gallon of gas produces 20 pounds of carbon dioxide, which contains five pounds of pure carbon. It is, says environmental writer John Ryan, "like tossing a five-pound bag of charcoal briquettes out [the] window every 20 miles or so."

You do the math: There are 232 million cars in the United States, and 700 million or so in the world. We're expected to hit one billion by 2020—or maybe sooner. Populous China, a traditionally bike-oriented country, is starting to ban bikes in the streets of its cities and increasing car manufacturing annually.

If you do decide you need to buy a car, remember that small is beautiful. SUVs and pick-ups are gas-guzzlers. Hybrid vehicles can be a good choice, especially for city driving. The gas-electric combo engines get better mileage than conventional vehicles and emit fewer pollutants. Some carmakers are starting to produce "flex-fuel" vehicles, too, which can run on a gas-ethanol blend. And electric and hydrogen cars aren't far behind.

And keep in mind that a new car isn't the only option, or even the best—new cars can depreciate as much as 35% in the first year.

> AN ENGINEER IN CALIFORNIA WON THE "AMERICA'S LONGEST COMMUTE" TITLE IN 2006, WINNING $10,000 IN GAS MONEY FOR DRIVING 186 MILES TO WORK EACH DAY—AND 186 MILES HOME.

Dare to Share

Car sharing is an organized way to share the environmental and economic burden of automobile use—with complete strangers. You don't have to do the organizing: car-sharing businesses have sprung up around the country and the world. The cars are maintained and insured by someone else, and, depending on your locale, may be hybrids or even cute little MINIs. Doesn't that sound divine?

Generally, you pay a membership fee plus mileage and/or hourly fees when you use a car. For example, at Flexcar, one of the most popular car-share services, an annual membership fee is usually about $35 per year. You choose a rate plan with fees that range from $9 per hour to anywhere from $75 to $700 per month, depending on how much you want to drive. Not so pricey, huh? You probably pay the equivalent of a midrange car-sharing rate for your car insurance alone, not counting the costs of purchasing a car, making repairs, and filling the tank.

And with shared cars, you don't have to worry about any of that. The cars are parked in neighborhoods around the city. You just reserve one near your home and return it on time when you're done. In short, car sharing offers all the convenience of a personal automobile without the hassle. If you join a program that uses hybrids, you get twice as much bang for your eco-buck: an efficient car shared among one giant family. Take the leap.

According to the American Council for an Energy-Efficient Economy's (ACEEE) Green Book—an annual ranking not to be missed by anyone curious about cleaner cars—manufacturing accounts for 9% of a car's lifetime energy use, so buying used can cut down on the impact of your purchase. Just be sure the beater you pick is new enough to be safe, get decent mileage, and have emissions-control systems.

For more info on the environmentally sound way to evaluate your current car or choose a new one, consult the ACEEE, the Department of Energy, or Tom and Ray from National Public Radio's *Car Talk* (*www.cartalk.com*). Just don't drive like their brother.

FOR THIS RELIEF, MUCH TANKS

You've probably been hearing more and more about biofuels as an option for avoiding the oil industry and generally saving the world. But what exactly are they? Very simply, they are fuels derived from vegetation.

Biofuels are increasingly being hailed by engine tinkerers and world leaders alike because they burn cleaner than oil. And while oil tends, perhaps because of the wealth and power it confers on its controllers, to be concentrated in politically unstable areas, the feedstock for biofuel literally springs from the ground beneath our feet. The two types currently getting lots of folks excited are biodiesel and ethanol.

Biodiesel is basically vegetable oil—made from soy, rapeseed, palm oil, or even used restaurant grease—that is compatible with diesel engines. Cars using biodiesel get the same mileage as those fueled by conventional diesel—which is to say, a lot—while emitting less CO_2, less sulfur, and less particulate matter. Translation: Biodiesel-fueled vehicles contribute less to climate change and air pollution. Plus, you get that eau-du-french-fry exhaust.

An alcohol-based fuel usually made from sugar cane or corn, **ethanol** has been embraced in Brazil and is gaining steam in the United States. (Yes, you can drink it in its purest form, but we don't advise it.) If you haven't encountered E85 fuel yet—a blend of 85 percent ethanol and 15 percent gaso-line—you might soon: it is available at hundreds of filling stations nationwide, and the push is on to expand its reach. You need a flex-fuel vehicle to burn E85, but most petroleum-powered cars can use a 10% ethanol blend.

While these fuels are popular alternatives to petroleum, manufacturing them requires boosting agricultural production.

And that's where the sustainability argument starts to fall a little short. Critics worry that all this emphasis on growing crops for fuel will mean less food for the

You Want Me to Put What into My Tank?

Corn and soy seem like reasonable sources for fuel. But turkey beaks, greasy pizza boxes, and pond scum? All three are being studied as possible tank-fillers, as are pig poop, paper waste, and human and animal fat. Um, we'll just walk, thanks.

The U.S. Environmental Protection Agency National Vehicle and Fuel Emissions Laboratory and the California Air Resources Board confirm that when given the choice of idling for a few minutes or turning your car off, you should always choose the latter. Tests comparing emissions over minute-long increments for restarted versus idled cars confirm: idling produces more emissions. Over nine minutes, for example, an idling car will emit double the pollutants of a car that is turned off and then restarted. Of course, it depends on the car you're driving and other variables, but you can feel confident turning off your engine for any delays longer than a minute.

world to eat, more abuse of land and water through industrial agriculture, and more genetically modified crops. Moreover, simply changing what we burn in the internal combustion engine will not magically solve all the problems posed by the passenger car.

GETTING RID OF YOUR RIDE

The best reason to get rid of a car is simple: owning vehicles encourages their use. Whether you have one car or three, you are contributing emissions that cause planetary problems. If you had one less vehicle, you and your family might be inclined to arrange a ride share, or combine trips, or go to a store that's closer to home. You might lobby your local politicians to make the roads safer for bicycles. You might use some of the money you'd normally put into car insurance, gas, and upkeep to buy an electric bike or scooter and brave the roads.

You can trade your car in or sell it to a needy teenager, but a donation might have higher worth. Explore local charities that accept cars and ask your friendly neighborhood accountant what you'll be able to deduct if you donate.

Sing the Chassis Electric

The climate is right for electric cars, and several automakers are rolling out new models. It's "an untapped market that is phenomenal," says the CEO of ZAP, a California-based company that introduced the three-wheel electric Xebra in 2006 (yes, it comes zebra-striped). While low-speed, relatively low-price vehicles like Miles Automotive's ZX40 and the Tomberlin Group's E-Merge E-2 are hitting the road, it's the sports cars that are getting the most attention. The swanky Tesla Roadster (with a $98,000 price tag) is only the start: Wrightspeed Inc. is developing a $100,000 sports car that could go up to 120 mph and run for 200 miles between charges, and Phoenix Motorcars will sell two 85-mph, 120-miles-per-charge cars. Companies estimate that charging an electric car costs a mere one to three cents per mile. Actress and electric-car plugger Alexandra Paul says the new models will defy the idea "that an electric car is pokey or doesn't have range." And if a *Baywatch* babe says it, you know it must be true.

The United States Environmental Protection Agency (EPA) says 10.5 million cars "reach the end of their useful lives" in the United States each year. If your car ends up getting junked, consider it a desirable source of reusable materials. Your trusty steed will be gutted, with fluids drained and useful organs such as alternators, tires, transmission, and seats removed for resale. Next, crushing! Your giant car becomes a dense cube. The cube is then shredded, and the shreds are sorted.

The EPA also estimates that 75% of each car's weight is recycled, which is impressive. But it's that other 25% that's the trouble. Despite this residue's fun name—auto fluff!—it is the main downside to your reprocessed vehicle. It has no easy use, can contain toxins such as mercury and lead, and usually ends up in a landfill. Check out the Clean Car Campaign (*www.cleancarcampaign.org*) to learn more about putting the brakes on use of these nasties in the car-manufacturing process.

For inspiration we look to Europe, which has induced vehicle manufacturers to assume end-of-life responsibility for their products. Maybe it's easier to recycle a Renault?

AT THE CARWASH (WHOA, WHOA, WHOA)

We like to pretend the most responsible car wash is no car wash at all, but that's because we're lazy sods. In truth, keeping your car clean of grime and salt can help prolong its life, which keeps you out of the car-consumption game.

So what's the best way to wash? Doing it at home might be cheaper and handier, but it's nearly always better to go to the commercial car wash. By mixing air and water half and half, car wash businesses use 60% less water in the entire process than you use just rinsing off your car! U.S. commercial car washes are also required to send their used water off for treatment, or to take other measures that lessen the impacts of their discharge. Some of them even reuse their water.

Home washes, on the other hand, waste approximately 116 gallons of water, which usually drains directly to storm sewers, eventually emptying into streams, lakes, rivers, or bays, adversely affecting our fish friends and their habitat.

A survey by the International Carwash Association (really!) found that a little under half of Americans prefer to suds up in the driveway, though. So if you do decide to keep washing the car at home, here are a few tips.

> Try not to do it very often.

> If you can, park the car on your lawn, which acts as a natural filter for the soap, dirt, oil, and other gunk that would otherwise run straight into storm drains. (Of course, you might not want that stuff on your lawn, either; see first tip.)

> Use less water by buying a nozzle that controls the flow from your hose or by using a bucket—this will help you keep an eye on how much you're using.

> Collect rainwater or lightly used water (like the soapy stuff in your dishwashing bin) from your house and wash with that.

> Try an eco-friendly soap like Dr. Bronner's, or no soap at all. The detergents in regular car cleaners hurt fish, and even those labeled biodegradable and low-phosphate can make our fish friends unhappy.

> The average American spends more than 1.5 hours in the car every day.
> There are 232 million registered vehicles in the United States, and 300 million people.
> Average fuel economy for automobiles has fallen 5% in the past 20 years, from a high of 22.1 in 1987 to 21 today.
> Though Americans spend just 6% of the day commuting on average, that time is responsible for 60% of their daily exposure to fine-particle pollution.
> Cars and light trucks in the United States account for 43% of the country's oil consumption, and 11% of the world's oil consumption.
> In the United States, 40,000 people a year die in traffic accidents.
> The average car emits 12,000 pounds of carbon dioxide each year.
> Underinflated tires can cause a 5% decrease in fuel economy.
> Cars and light trucks in the United States traveled a combined 2.7 trillion miles in 2004—the equivalent of 10 million trips to the moon.

HEIGH HO, HEIGH HO, IT'S OFF
TO WORK YOU GO

With the possible exception of Grumpy, the Seven Dwarfs seemed awfully complacent about heading to work in a diamond mine. Perhaps all that incessant whistling blocked out the environmental horrors of the mining industry? With any luck, your job is a little kinder to the earth. But if you're working in an office, there are countless things you can do to reduce the footprint your business makes. (Hint: Whistling isn't one of them.)

THINK NORMA RAE, BE NORMA RAE

If you're environmentally minded, working in an office whose policies don't include recycling can drive you to the brink. One way to deal with all that frustration is to channel it into a personal campaign to change your building's wicked ways.

Begin by gathering persuasive information about the benefits of mixed-paper recycling. Call your local solid-waste agency and ask them for resources, advice, and good news about the bottom line of companies that recycle. What you are looking for are little inspirational sayings, such as, "After an initial investment to set up the system, recycling can often reduce garbage costs for businesses." Ask similar-sized companies in the area if they recycle and what makes it worthwhile for them. Pump them for more uplifting quotes, e.g., "We actually make a little money from selling our recyclables, and we use it to buy Tootsie Pops for everyone on staff."

Meanwhile, back on the frontlines, convince your cubicle cohorts that sorting trash is the best office entertainment since Tetris. When you have gathered plenty of support and plenty of statistics, you are ready to campaign. Find an approachable, influential person in the corporation—your supervisor, say, or the office manager—and meet with him or her. Present your persuasive, cost-effective, easy-to-institute plan for institutional recycling—and while you're at it, make a cheerful inquiry into buying recycled paper. You must be nice, reasonable, positive, and patient. Don't complain. Offer to help. Victory will be yours.

One Ringy-Dingy, Two Ringy-Dingy

Internet access is widely heralded as a tool with the potential to transform the lives of low-income people around the world, but construction of a wired network to remote villages is often prohibitively expensive. Enter the Green Wi-Fi project, which has developed a solar-powered wireless router that can run for up to four weeks even in prolonged periods of gray skies. Another organization aiming to increase global communication is ReCellular. With about 53% of the U.S. phone-recycling market, the company keeps some 75,000 functional cell phones out of landfills every week, many of which it refurbishes and sells in developing countries. Says ReCellular Vice President Mike Newman, "The fact that you can combine a business—a profitable business—with a useful service and a charitable good is a win, win, win." We're guessing you know a few people with old cell phones to spare. Why not start a collection drive at work?

RE-BOOT CAMP

Electronic waste is a big, big problem. Computers are nifty, and it's astounding how we went from a model as big as a room to one smaller than our hand in a few decades. But here's how we did it: using lead, cadmium, mercury, PVC, beryllium, and other environmental evils. One result of galloping technological innovation is piles of these and other useful, persistent, bioaccumulative toxins in our incinerators and landfills. It's a short hop from piles in landfills to piles in our livers.

So save this information for the day when the computer screen upon which you gaze for hours upon hours no longer suits your needs. The National Recycling Coalition's list of electronics-recycling programs by state will get you started. If you can't find anything local, the major manufacturers—Apple, Gateway, Dell, Hewlett-Packard, and IBM—all have various take-back and trade-in programs. (Even eBay has gotten into the act.)

If you are willing to spread the electronics-recycling gospel—and it is a worthy task—the Computer TakeBack Campaign (*www.computertakeback.com*) gives an excellent summary. Office workers can do a world of good by insisting on a decent computer end-of-life plan at your jobs and you can apply the info to your home computer as well.

Once again, Europe has a jump on the United States when it comes to regulations: The European Union enacted two major electronic-waste laws in recent years that restrict use of hazardous substances and mandate recovery of gadgets. Several countries in Asia, too, have tightened up on both manufacturing and disposal. The rest of us must just promise to be responsible.

There's a nasty rumor persisting in the land of PCs: It purports that leaving your computer in sleep mode all night uses less energy than turning it on and off every morning and night. But it just isn't true! Turning off your computer at the end of the day is the way to go. Extinguishing that little green light reduces heat and mechanical stress and prolongs the machine's life, so you'll be saving energy and money, as well as postponing the day it's time to recycle your trusty techno-sidekick. If you leave your computer on so your data will get backed up, store sensitive files on a company server instead, or talk to your pals in IT about performing backups during the day instead of at night.

While you're working, you can save energy by encouraging your computer to sleep as often as possible, and using the sleep mode instead of a screensaver. But at the end of the day, turn the thing off. Or even better, hit it with a sledgehammer, pack up your desk, and go work on an organic vegetable farm.

A Real Turn-Off

YOUR LIGHTS ARE ON

In the course of your daily meanderings, you're likely to be faced with the lights-on/lights-out debate. Some people contend that turning the lights on and off demands more energy than just leaving them on all the time. But here's a simple rule to remember whenever the controversy pops up: think of Lady Macbeth. *Out! Out!*

Turn out the lights if you are the last to leave a room, unless you are coming back within two minutes. Contrary to popular belief, turning lights on consumes no more electricity than they use when already lit. This is true for both fluorescent and incandescent bulbs. *Out! Out!*

Fluorescent lights do have a finite number of starts built into the ballast, the mechanism in the bulb that translates electricity into illumination. But in order to wear out the ballast before the rest of the bulb burns out, you would need to turn your lights on and off twenty to fifty times a day. So. *Out!* Even in the office bathroom.

If you're wondering about those fluorescent tubes hanging above your head, know this; they are highly efficient and hence a good option for the environment. If you don't like the quality of light they cast, you may have old light fixtures that reflect light poorly, or you may just have older fluorescent tubes that have been up there forever (because they're so efficient, remember?). Modern fixtures and well-chosen tubes should result in well-lit, warm, energy-efficient spaces. Look into compact fluorescent lights (CFLs), which are 75% more energy efficient than incandescent lights and last longer too.

EARNING GREEN BY WORKING GREEN

Warning! A commitment to being green at the office may well morph into a larger quest: the desire to work at an "environmental job." The environmental careers market is strong and steady right now, not only in traditional fields like environmental protection and natural-resource management, but in the rapidly expanding world of organics, renewable energy, energy conservation/efficiency, environmental health, green building, and research areas related to global warming. But beyond "VP of Tree Planting" and "Ozone Repairman," exactly what qualifies as an environmental job?

Long, long ago, in an almost forgotten age (before the Internet, before cable television, even before *Dancing with the Stars),* environmental jobs were synonymous with an easily identifiable group of people: wildlife biologists, park rangers, wastewater technicians, foresters, sanitarians, land-use planners, certain engineers, geologists, agricultural scientists, marine ecologists, a few niche lawyers, and the occasional recycling coordinator.

All of these professions are still with us, but in the current lexicon, the adjective "environmental" has lost its limited land, air, and water definition. The term has also morphed into other adjectives—"sustainable," "green," and "eco-"—that get attached to professions like accounting, marketing, journalism, and architecture. With no accepted definition to depend upon, estimates of the number of "environmental" jobs in the nation have ranged from as few as 400,000 to as many as 4 million or more.

As industries like agriculture, transportation, construction, manufacturing, finance, energy, communications, tourism, and consumer products struggle to become more sustainable, the greatest environmental contributions are often made by people far outside of the "environmental" department whose training has often had very little direct environmental content.

The crummy thing about work is that you aren't guaranteed to be toiling alongside people whose politics—environmental or otherwise—are in line with yours. Most of the time unpleasant clashes can be avoided ("How 'bout those [insert local sports team here]?"), but this becomes tricky when you can so readily see ways to green your office.

If you can't resist giving your fellow cube-izens a little eco-education, we'd strongly advise against donning a hemp suit, clambering up on a breakroom table, and condemning the absence of natural fibers in the carpeting. Nobody likes getting preached to at work, especially when they're trying to eat lunch.

Instead, try one of the environmental "elevator pitches" suggested by Grist readers. These are digestible, pro-eco arguments that can be made in the space of an elevator ride. (Though if we were rocking our hemp suit we'd recommend taking the stairs, to save energy.) Pick your favorite, or experiment to see which seems the most convincing. Who knows, pretty soon you may no longer be an eco-army of one.

1. Environmentalism is society's way of keeping the toilet from backing up. Without it we'd be awash in our own poop.

2. Environmentalism is waking up every day breathing clean air, drinking safe water, eating healthy food, having a real vote, and knowing that your grandkids—and theirs—will too.

3. Think of the Earth as a great bank whose funds are natural beauty and resources. Environmentalists are certified financial advisors. They give free advice about maintaining and increasing our wealth. »

4. Environmentalism is a way of ensuring your grandchildren aren't hideous, three-eyed monsters who are hungry, and slowly, painfully dying of mercury poisoning in a vast wasteland stripped of color and life.

5. Our survival in this elevator depends upon its being well maintained; likewise, our survival on this planet depends upon our maintenance of its resources.

6. Environmentalism is about life extension. It's cheaper than cryonics and you don't have to die first.

7. Do you love breathing air and drinking water? Mountains, oceans, cities, streams? Want kids to grow up healthy, happy, and peaceful? That's environmentalism. It's about everyone and everything you love.

Old definitions have disappeared, but new ones have yet to emerge. We're left with questions. If you have a doctorate in earth science but spend your days ripping up the planet, are you still an environmental professional? And what about people who sell organic herbal shampoos?

On the road to an environmentally sound economy, we'll see a spectrum of environmental jobs. Whether you're hunting or hiring, we suggest asking the following five questions to measure the "degree of environmentalness" for real jobs in the real world:

1. What is the intention/mission of the employing institution?

2. What measurable sustainability results is the employing institution achieving?

3. What is the impact/role of the specific job toward sustainability results?

4. What is the importance of environmentally related training/education on the job?

5. What is the conscious intention of the person in the job?

Applying these questions, we would find (for example) that a committed environmentalist (#5), educated and employed as a conservation biologist (#4), responsible for managing (#3) a successful, ecosystem-scale protection project that also creates jobs for low-income residents (#2) at Conservation International (#1) would rank at the higher end of the spectrum of "environmentalness."

We would also find, however, that there might be a lot of #5 and #4, but only a little of #1, #2, and #3. Still an environmental job? You bet.

You can play at home! What's the environmentalness quotient of your job, or the one you aspire to? Where do you draw the line? Which factors count for a lot, and which are less important?

CRAZY LITTLE THING CALLED LUNCH

Lunch! What a great invention! Such a nice break, smack dab in the middle of the day—an authorized excuse to step away from your grueling routine. As a concept, lunch needs little in the way of improvement. But as you might expect, being thoughtful about how you engage in this edible endeavor can make the midday respite even more of a treat.

WHO'S ON SECONDS?

One of the central tenets of living green is to reduce consumption whenever and wherever possible. In fact, a long-held lunchtime tradition fits perfectly within the consumption-reduction guidelines. No, not the three-martini lunch—we're talking about leftovers! Reheating what you didn't finish the night before is the perfect way to avoid having to buy plastic-wrapped, mass-produced, shipped-from-who-knows-where sustenance.

> AMERICANS, ON AVERAGE, SPEND HALF THEIR FOOD BUDGET ON MEALS MADE OUTSIDE THE HOME.

So how best to transport last night's culinary treasures? We admit we have a soft spot for airtight convenience, but plastic is not the best choice, healthwise. Before Tupperware became omnipresent, workers and students transported food in containers made from other materials. Perhaps you remember ye olde metal lunchboxes? They aren't just for kids! Your trusty lunch pail need not be emblazoned with Spiderman or Dora; the classic "construction worker" model can be both sleek and sexy.

Thinking inside the box, try using old-school strategies to wrap your food. Waxed paper can be used for sandwiches (either tie it with string or secure it with rubber bands). Loosely enfold cookies and carrots in butcher paper or napkins, the latter of which can be handily reused to wipe the crumbs from your shirtfront. Add a thermos of soup, and you've got a retro-chic lunch pail. Martha Stewart *wishes*.

Judging by their titles, you'd think the following characters might have held green jobs. But are these high-profile hires true eco-peeps or posers?

> **Mr. Green Jeans** (Captain Kangaroo's right-hand man)
> > Handyman (recycler) and friend to all animals.
> > Wore same pair of overalls everyday (anti-consumption).
> > Verdict: True Green.

> **Mean Joe Greene** (Noted Pittsburgh Steeler and star of 1970s
> > Coca Cola commercials)
> > After he so famously chugged that Coke, did he recycle
> > the bottle?
> > Verdict: Postgame analysis needed.

> **The Jolly Green Giant** (Spokesmodel for Green Giant Food Company)
> > Dresses entirely in leaves (sustainably harvested?).
> > Skin tone questionable (from exposure to high
> > fructose corn syrup?).
> > Pushes vegetables on children (but they're canned).
> > Been around since 1928 (must be living healthy).
> > Verdict: Too close to cauliflower.

> **The Green Hornet** (Masked Crusader)
> > Drove gigantic, souped-up, gas-guzzling Chrysler Imperial to all
> > crime scenes, even those that were a walkable distance.
> > Verdict: Faux Green.

FOILED AGAIN

Another option you might consider for your lunchtime leftover needs is aluminum foil. Using foil isn't as egregious as you might think (unless you accidentally get some in your fillings—yeow). But there are some important things to know about tinfoil in order to avoid its curses.

The mining and processing of aluminum (or, as history and the Brits would have it, aluminium) is extremely resource intensive. This is ameliorated only by the fact that aluminum is practically 100% recyclable, and does not degrade as it is recycled—apparently, it can be reworked into infinity without losing quality. Plastic, by contrast, loses quality each time it is recycled, and eventually must be chucked. So we love recycling aluminum. Here's just one motivational factoid: Americans are said to throw away enough aluminum in three months to rebuild our entire commercial air fleet.

Aluminum foil is technically just as recyclable as aluminum cans. It's just that we often make foil dirtier than cans, and many recycling programs will not accept it due to this problem. You may wish to double-check with your local recycling peeps and see what would happen if you gave your foil a nice wipe or rinse to remove the BBQ sauce before sending it to them. It's also possible that you could wash the foil and reuse it, treating it more like a pot or a pan.

(One downer about aluminum: while the foil you use for leftovers is a visible example of this precious, energy-intensive commodity, aluminum is also used as a layer in many types of lightweight packaging—aseptic soy milk and juice boxes being one example—which typically can't be recycled.)

If you are unable to recycle foil in your area, and you are reducing and reusing to the best of your ability, there's one more way to make the situation better: buy recycled foil. There are 100% recycled-content brands available. The recycling process uses about 5% of the energy of the original processing. That is a big difference, so buying recycled foil is a worthwhile endeavor. If you can't get it easily in your neck of the woods, order some online.

REHEAT WAVE

If you work in an office there's little hope of escaping the telltale hum and ding of the lunchroom microwave, doing its magical warming business all day long. The good news is, despite popular parlance, microwaves are not nuclear—and

If traditional lunch boxes aren't your thing, try thinking globally. Explore Asian markets for a slick, three-tiered Indian lunch pail called a *tiffin*. Three flat-bottomed metal bowls stack together, the second providing a lid for the first, the third providing a lid for the second. The third and top bowl has its own lid, which locks into position with the flip of a latch. It transports liquid, semisolid, and solid foods with nary an incident. And it's way cool. For those bereft of nearby Asian markets, check out *www.ImportFood.com* or similar websites.

Boxes
Without
Borders

in fact, like toaster ovens, they're an efficient way to heat small portions (like lunch). The downside? Those mysterious spatters left inside by coworkers.

Here's what happens inside a microwave oven: A "magnetron" element produces "microwave"-band electromagnetic radiation, which bounces about on the oven walls. It penetrates food, hits the water molecules inside, and—no kidding—spins them around, causing them to rub up against one another. The food becomes heated as the rubbing spreads throughout, but the oven itself does not heat.

The magnetron emits electromagnetic radiation only when the oven is operating. When that minute-and-a-half is over and the microwave dings, the magnetron shuts off. Two separate locks must unlock to permit you inside the cavity for casserole retrieval: the double-locked vault protects you from the fury of Magnetron. You're in a science-fiction movie every time you use the oven!

Microwave ovens are more efficient than our familiar old friends, the electric and gas range/oven combos. Not only are microwave ovens faster, they use electricity more efficiently (efficiency in this instance being a measure of energy going to the food versus energy wasted), because the magnetron doesn't need to heat the ambient air.

As for whether you should be worried about stray radiation, the U.S. Food and Drug Administration (FDA) avers that radiation levels within two inches of standard microwave ovens are well below harmful standards. Two feet out, radiation is barely detectable. They also acknowledge, however, that no long-term studies have been done on exposure to these home appliance radiation levels. If you don't trust the FDA and its safety levels, consider these safety tips:

> Don't sit on, straddle, or lick your microwave while it's operating. Keep your distance.

> Teach kids how to use it safely.

> Use only glass or ceramic containers rather than plastic, to avoid meltdowns and potential leaching of chemicals into your foods.

> Don't use a microwave with a mangled door seal, and don't puncture or scratch the inside. Don't operate your microwave empty—all that unabsorbed energy can damage ye olde magnetron tube.

> Don't overheat water; it can superheat and burble up to scald you.

> If your oven has an electronic display, unplug it when you're not using it and you'll save quite a bit of money over the year—enough to go out to dinner.

Ding!

BEFORE YOU BITE THAT APPLE

Bringing fruit to work is a good and good-for-you idea, and one that might even help you avoid the siren song of the candy machine. But while it's convenient to reach into your lunchbox and take a bite, take the extra step to walk down the hall and give it a good rinse first. Internal contamination from pesticides, herbicides, waxes, and the wages of sin won't be washed away, but some external contamination will.

Think about your produce. It may have traveled from Mexico, China, California, or Chile. It was picked, cleaned, cut, and packed by a giant diesel machine or tired humans. It was shipped hundreds if not thousands of miles, in proximity with other, unknown, commodities. It was unloaded from the truck, unpacked from the box, and placed on the display, where it sat for a few hours or days as hundreds of people walked by, leaning over it, breathing on it, and touching it. Who knows how many other hands have fondled your broccoli, or how many germy miasmas have wafted past each floret. Mmm, still hungry?

Given our current food-distribution matrix, it's a miracle that so few health disasters happen. Hepatitis A, like other yucky food-borne illnesses such as E. coli and campylobacter, has a fecal–oral transmission route. The feces in question can be from animal compost, tainted water, or human hands. That's why hand-washing is vital at every stage of food production, transport, and consumption. Washing produce in the kitchen is also an important factor in reducing the possibility of food-borne illness. Even if you buy local, you should wash your food (especially since farm-fresh local produce often carries the pesticide-free seal in the form of dirt and slugs).

This need to treat your baby carrots as a potential disease vector has very clear environmental connections, as food-safety hazards are harder to control and trace in a global food system. Although the United States has high environmental and food-handling standards, our food is often grown far from inspectors and fines, not to mention clean water. The system by which food is grown and shipped to the United States includes ill effects like fossil-fuel consumption, pesticide contamination of workers and water, loss of species diversity, destruction of wilderness lands, devastation of farming communities, the creation of a large mobile population turned out from their traditional land-based occupations, and on and on.

All this reinforces the importance of supporting local agriculture (which we'll talk more about when dinnertime rolls around). If you work in an office with a cafeteria, talk to the food service manager to see how you can get more local foods incorporated into the offerings. And when your boss asks why you're spending so much time in the cafeteria, tell her you're only thinking of her health.

THE TAKE ON TAKE-OUT

We know it's simply not always possible to bring your lunch to work, so if you must take out, take into account what we know about those ubiquitous foam containers. (And hey, easy on those paper napkins.)

Prefer Your Bottles in V-Neck or Cardigan?

In California alone, some 3 million plastic bottles go unrecycled every day. The empty containers enter the waste stream, where they take up space in landfills or are incinerated, yielding toxic fumes. If recycled, that quantity of bottles could be used to make 74 million square feet of carpet—or 16 million sweaters.

First, a little factoid: what you refer to as Styrofoam likely isn't.

Styrofoam is the trademarked name of the Dow Chemical Company's exclusive blue extruded polystyrene insulation. What we call Styrofoam is actually expanded polystyrene, known as EPS. It's made by heating polystyrene particles, pouring them into molds, and injecting them with steam. Meat trays, coffee cups, picnic coolers, and their ilk are all made from EPS, never from Styrofoam. Of course, being particular about saying EPS instead of Styrofoam may be one of those uphill battles, like saying "hook-and-loop fabric adhesive" instead of "Velcro" and "flying disc" instead of "Frisbee."

While Styrofoam became infamous back in the 1980s for the ozone-depleting chemicals used in its manufacture, making EPS never involved CFCs. But should you avoid it? There is some debate in the environmental community about whether EPS is an ecologically good or bad product choice. Because it is derived from petroleum, it is not a renewable resource, and it is completely nonbiodegradable. Industry advocates consider this a selling point, as that means EPS will not leach any nasty chemicals into landfills. Talk about a silver lining. Solid-waste experts are still unclear as to whether it is better to use products made from paper or EPS.

Until a solid consensus arrives, carry on in a sensible manner, avoiding packaging and disposable containers of all sorts as much as possible. If you're having trouble figuring out how to transport your Phad Thai in your bare hands, accept the EPS box and balance it out by keeping a set of silverware and cloth napkins in your desk drawer.

If you're dashing out for lunch (on foot, we hope!), try to skip the standard fast-food fare; the industrial agriculture and chemicals behind it are cruddy for both your health and the land.

"As a consumer, you can think of each purchase as a vote," *Fast Food Nation* author Eric Schlosser has told Grist. "When you go to fast-food chains and buy industrial meat, you're endorsing those practices. If you spend a little more time and money and buy food that's being produced the right way by conscientious people, then you're supporting a totally different system."

While these joints may not be 100% green, they are at least making the effort to bring healthier lunches to the hungry masses:

> Burger King (*www.burgerking.com*): In early 2007, the chain made a whopper of a splash by announcing that it would begin buying sustainably raised eggs and pork
> Burgerville (*www.burgerville.com*): This Northwest chain uses antibiotic- and hormone-free, humanely raised beef
> Chipotle (*www.chipotle.com*): Buys organic beans and sustainably raised pork, and is expanding its verde ventures
> McDonald's (*www.mcdonalds.com*): The Golden Arch folks dole out organic coffee, milk, and meat in some locations, and have made milk and fruit available for Happy Meals.
> O'Naturals (*www.onaturals.com*): All-natural, organic cafe created by the founders of Stonyfield Farm has a handful of locations in Maine, Massachusetts, Kansas, and Florida.
> Organic To Go (*www.organictogo.com*): A West Coast caterer with a taste for pesticide-free plates.
> Panera Bread (*www.panerabread.com*): Ubiquitous eatery serves antibiotic-free chicken and organic kids' meals.
> Whole Foods (*www.wholefoods.com*): OK, you got us, it's not a restaurant—but the prepared foods section is to salivate for.

BOTTLENECK

More and more, the water cooler is being replaced by individual water bottles, with many companies stocking them in the fridge as an office perk. But there's nothing perky about bottled water.

In short: bottled water is almost entirely unregulated, and studies have shown that some bottled water has more bacteria and chemicals than tap water. Bottling water from springs (water mining) can have a devastating effect on ecosystems. Also, the containers release dangerous toxic chemicals into the air and water when they are manufactured and when they are burned or buried. Feeling thirsty? There's more.

About 1.5 million tons of plastic are used to create water bottles each year. (Think of how we could improve our tap-water infrastructure if we took the money spent on bottled water and spent it on our public water systems.) As we know, manufacturing plastic is resource intensive and yields various evil emissions that contribute to global warming and degradation of water quality.

Instead of fretting about plastic resins and trying to keep all the numbers straight, pass right over the entire issue by using a different material. In most situations, you do not even need a plastic water container. If you're at a desk, or in the kitchen, or even at spinning class, glass or ceramic vessels are fine (Grizzly Adams types may favor a metal canteen). There is no good reason to use plastic water bottles in everyday life unless you are a professional cyclist or mountain climber.

While you're munching on your midday meal, take a moment to consider the children—even if you don't have any—and the flavorless, high-fructose corn syrup-drenched, nutritionally suspect convenience food unceremoniously plopped on trays all over the country. Never known to be mouth watering, school lunches have plunged to a culinary nadir in recent years. The dire situation is outlined in the book *Lunch Lessons: Changing the Way We Feed Our Children*, by Ann Cooper. A former star chef, Cooper now proudly styles herself a "renegade lunch lady" on a mission to transform the nation's abysmal school-lunch system.

While the national school-lunch program originally started from an urgent need to counter rampant malnutrition, it now needs a complete overhaul to combat a new scourge: surging diabetes and obesity rates. According to Cooper, 78% of schools in America do not actually meet the USDA's nutritional guidelines. It's no wonder, really: as she points out, school cafeterias have $2.40 per day to spend on each kid—70% of which goes to payroll and overhead. That leaves 72 cents to spend on ingredients. (All in all, the U.S. government spends about $7 billion per year on school lunches— roughly equal to a month's worth of military expenditures in the Iraq war.)

Given those Dickensian financial constraints, it's also no wonder that over the last 30 years, schools have replaced trained cooks with de-skilled workers and abandoned cooking for reheating. »

When Cooper took the job as nutrition director of the Berkeley Unified School System in 2005, she found that the district's food-service system had completely retreated from actual cooking.

"When I arrived, 100% of the food arrived in plastic, was reheated in plastic, and [was] served to the kids in plastic," she says. Overcoming an absurdly stringent budget and severely limited cooking infrastructure within school cafeterias, she is now serving fresh, made-from-scratch meals. But she has no intention of stopping there. She would like to overthrow the logic that has made school cafeterias conduits through which convenience-food manufacturers reach children's impressionable palates and encourages parents to find out just what their kids are wolfing down.

For the infrequent times when nothing but a lightweight, unbreakable material will do, set aside a plastic bottle made with #2, #4, or #5 plastic (the numbers are on the bottom). But please note: If you're making an effort to reduce water bottle consumption by using the same one over and over, know that reused, unwashed, and unsterilized plastic bottles are a breeding ground for invisible bacteria that nestle in cracks and scratches we cannot even see. This threat isn't as exotic as the fancy chemicals found in plastic, but it is gross.

ONE TRAY AT A TIME

"Got anything green to eat?" It's probably not a question you hear much around your company's cafeteria, but you might soon. A growing number of companies are thinking about the environmental impacts of the food they serve employees. And along the way, institutional food is being replaced by cuisine that won't bite the land that feeds you.

Some companies are buying seasonal, local produce and locally produced baked goods, which supports the regional economy and reduces the impacts of transporting food. They are looking out for organic or fair-trade certified labels. They are putting hormone- and antibiotic-free poultry, livestock, and dairy products, as well as sustainably harvested seafood, on the table—to protect employees' health, and the health of the planet's other inhabitants.

The greening of food service has been taking place for some time in colleges and universities, where students have demanded foods that align with their environmental, political, and social interests. Colorado College's campus cafeteria, for instance, started an "organic when possible" service that features free-range turkey sausage, vegan pizza, and certified-organic fries.

Now similar stories are coming from corporate campuses, including those of Adidas, Amgen, Cisco, Google, Intel, and Nordstrom. The Clif Bar headquarters in Berkeley, California, offers an Amy's Kitchen vending machine on-site, featuring organic frozen entrees. The Sustainable Food Center sets up lunchtime farmers' markets to allow Austinites to buy locally grown food.

Could it happen at your workplace?

CLICK TO BUY

Shopping is a favorite lunch-hour activity for many of us. After all, it can have the same nourishing effect as food ... all those delicious sweaters and tasty shoes! Thanks to modern technology, you can shop quickly and (relatively) guilt-free on the Internet, without ever turning on your car.

But my DVDs are shipped, you say!

Ah yes, but Internet shopping uses less energy to get a package to your house. Shipping a 10-pound package by overnight air— the most energy-intensive delivery mode—uses 40% less fuel than the average roundtrip drive to the mall. Ground shipping by truck uses just one-tenth the energy of a trip by car to the store.

In fact, each minute spent driving to the mall uses more than 10 times the energy of a minute spent shopping on the Internet. Online shopping eliminates the need for car trips and reduces congestion. People with Internet access say they go to the store or the mall less often, and about 77% of American households shop online.

A Catalog of Ills

Welcome to the land of catalogs, where you can find everything from leg-massaging chairs to butt-enhancing briefs. Even when they're peddling stuff we actually want, catalogs flood our lives too often, too thickly, and too glossily. Only 2 to 4% of catalogs mailed actually produce an order, but they are just successful enough at seducing us to keep the mail order business going. Catalog sales must be one of the world's most wasteful endeavors.

Let us be clear about what is being wasted: The trees and inks that go into the catalogs; the fuels that print, assemble, sort, label, bale, truck, and deliver them; the space in our kitchens or garages where we store them before more energy takes them to the recycling center or dump; and the extra costs that show up in our taxes (for the recycling or dump) and in the price of the product.

Of the 19 billion catalogs mailed every year to American consumers (that's 63 catalogs for each and every one of us!), very few—about 5%—contain any recycled materials. A group called Forest Ethics puts pressure on major companies to change their ways, and two of the biggest—Williams-Sonoma and Victoria's Secret—have agreed to use paper that's been certified as sustainable by the Forest Stewardship Council.

Take a hike through Forest Ethics (*www.forestethics.org*) to learn more about the underbelly of your shiny, happy catalogs. Take your name off of mailing lists by contacting companies or using a service like the Direct Marketing Association (*www.dmaconsumers.org*) or Greendimes (*www.greendimes.com*). And then take your shopping cart online!

You can reduce shopping guilt even further by using "socially responsible shopping" sites like *www.alonovo.com*. By way of corporate commissions with online giants like Amazon, these sites are able to contribute 20–40% of their revenue to the environmental cause of your choice. Which translates roughly as "shop til your emissions drop."

GYM DANDY

Even eco types like us can be couch potatoes (though the couch is formal-dehyde-free and our potatoes are organic and locally grown). But when the clock says 5:03 PM and the stress of your last meeting lingers on, nothing beats the satisfaction of a sweat-inducing, tension-releasing workout. (Well, that or a good stiff bourbon.) Still, popular modes of exercise come with their own set of environmental concerns, so educate yourself before dropping to give us twenty at the end of your busy day.

FOR THE FLEET OF FEET

Those of you whose post-work exercise routine includes an invigorating run may want to consider the implications of inhaling deeply—especially if you live and jog in an urban area.

Your chief outdoor foe is likely ozone, created when the chemicals in car exhaust and other emissions react to sun-light. It lurks mostly during the day, usually hitting its peak in the late afternoon and early evening, and lessens quickly as the sun goes down. Since traffic is usually lighter at night, and factories are likely to be spewing less, it's likely that nighttime air is cleaner than daytime air. Of course it all depends on weather, geography, traffic intensity, the type of pollution, and so on. Some particulate matter can stick around for weeks, but in general pollution weakens with time.

If your schedule—or safety concerns—don't allow for nighttime jogging, you still have options. Just pay attention to the local air-quality forecasts and keep a close eye on your body's reactions as you run, especially if you have asthma or another respiratory condition. Try not to run on days or nights when the air quality is especially bad. If you simply can't miss a day, ease up a bit: walk instead of jog, jog instead of sprint.

As for other alternatives, you could create a gym with your friends by combining collective equipment. Or think about joining a local sports league—you get to exercise and socialize all at once. (And whether you win or lose, there's always a reason to hoist an organic beer or two afterward.)

COME ON IN, THE WATER'S ... PROBABLY OKAY

We know some of you go to great lengths to achieve a weekly quota of laps at the pool. Perhaps you've noticed the scent of chlorine wafting off your skin for hours afterward and thought, "I stink of chemicals and my hair is turning brittle and green. Could this be harmful?"

Well, perk up those swimmer's ears as we dive into what we know about pools.

Chlorine is used to remove harmful contaminants from water, mostly because it's cheap (and because anyone who's swum in a kid-populated pool is thankful for its mighty pathogen-zapping powers). But when chlorine reacts with organic matter such as dirt and dandruff, a whole new family of chemicals results: trihalomethanes (THMs), which hang around in the water and the surrounding air. Their concentration depends on water temperature and the amount of chlorine in the pool.

When swimming in chlorinated water, you have an elevated exposure to this group of chemicals, though the actual risks from such exposure are currently unknown. How long do THMs persist in the body? In the case of the most notorious, chloroform, the answer appears to be: not very long. The U.S. Occupational Safety and Health Administration has set allowable workplace chloroform levels for the standard work week at 50 parts per million. Most pool air will be at that level or higher, but you are only in the pool for an hour or so.

If swimming is your exercise of choice (and if you don't do it all day long, every day), the associated chemicals aren't likely to do you in. Be aware that outdoor pools and indoor pools with high ceilings are considered safer than those in low-ceilinged or otherwise tight quarters. Rest assured that swimming is great exercise—and you look totally hot in that Speedo.

"GREEN GYMS"— VOLUNTEER CONSERVATION PROJECTS MARKETED AS OUTDOOR WORKOUTS—ARE A BOOMING TREND IN BRITAIN, AND HAVE EVEN BEEN RECOMMENDED BY DOCTORS.

Stairway to Heaven

Can't someone figure out a way to snatch up all those kilowatts you're creating by climbing that Stairmaster? Turns out they're on it.

Scientists and engineers are looking to make use of human-powered energy through means as unobtrusive as a matrix of pressure pads under sidewalks, floors, and treadmills. "When we walk along a pavement, eight watts of energy is wasted—absorbed by the ground—with each heel. Yet it's possible to harvest at least 30% of that energy," explains Claire Price, leader of the Pacesetters Project, which aimed to install the world's first human-energy-harvesting staircase in the United Kingdom in 2007. "[Human-powered energy] could power lighting, LED displays, and audio systems used in public spaces," she adds.

Another way you may soon be able to make yourself useful: a shoe device that would capture walking energy and use it to power portable electronic devices, being explored by the Massachusetts Institute of Technology.

Finally, how about this for two birds, one stone: Inventor Alex Gadsden has created a contraption called the Cyclean (*www.cyclean.biz*), which is a pedal-powered washing machine. Talk about clean energy!

GYM SHORTS

There's nothing quite like the sensation you have after a great workout. The endorphins are raging, the sweat is sticking, and you feel like Rocky— the Rocky from the first movie, no less. But here's the problem: gyms are huge energy gobblers—what with the cardio machines, the showers, the hair dryers, the air conditioning, and the immense loads of laundered towels. Plus the great majority of people drive to the gym, spending fossil fuels all the while. You may not be willing to drop your membership, but you might consider these other options:

LOW IMPACT

> Walk or bike to work.
> Run up and down the steps of your local museum (just *try* not to sing the *Rocky* theme song).
> Work in your garden.
> Do sit-ups while watching Animal Planet.
> Clean out your garage.
> Take your dog for a long walk.
> Chase your kids around the yard.

ADVANCED WORKOUT

› Bike home from the market with panniers full of fresh food.

› Volunteer to lift sacks of bulk grains at your grocery (you never know!).

› Join a group that clears trails in local hiking areas.

› Bench press your composting bin.

› Plant trees with a local arbor organization.

› Push a Hummer into a Prius car lot. Bonus workout: engage in the ensuing scuffle (don't forget to guard your face)!

Working Grist in Five Seconds or Less

Which of the following faced the most environmentally hazardous workplace?

A. Julia Roberts in *Erin Brockovich*
B. Meryl Streep in *Silkwood*
C. Charlize Theron in *North Country*
D. Sally Field in *Norma Rae*

The answer is E, none of the above. They're actresses! They only played endangered women on the screen.

A CONSUMPTION CENTERFOLD!

Sorry, no nudies here. Just some hot ideas for fleshing out your approach to being a smarter consumer.

We'll be the first to admit that consumption is one of life's great pleasures. Buying things we crave, traveling, eating delectable food, owning every Stevie Wonder album—it's all icing on the cake of life. But too often the effects of our blissful consumption aren't so sweet: pollution, emissions, and trash trail behind us.

Now consumption is getting even more complicated by the current wave of "eco-chic"—swanky, savvy people will tell you it's OK to buy things, as long as they're green things.

We think the truth lies somewhere in between. There's no need to swap pleasure for a barren, guilt-ridden existence. Nor does surrounding yourself with green gadgets and hemp handbags make you a better person. With thoughtfulness and commitment, consumption can be a force for good. Here's the naked truth: we consumers have the power to change how business is done.

To that end and for the future, here's a Consumption Proposition to tempt you:

ONE Reduce, Reuse, Recycle. It may sound as faded as Miss June 1962, but this brilliant triad still says it all. Reduce: Avoid buying what you don't need—and when you do buy new things, especially appliances, spend the money up front for an efficient model. Reuse: Buy used stuff, and wring the last drop of usefulness out of everything you own. Recycle: Do it, but remember that it only works in concert with the other two. Ultimately, recycling simply results in the manufacture of more things.

TWO Stay close to home. Work close to home to shorten your commute; eat food grown nearby; patronize local businesses; join neighborhood organizations.

THREE Internal combustion engines are polluting and their use should be minimized. Restrict all revving to your love machine!

FOUR Watch what you eat. Whenever possible, avoid food grown with pesticides, in feedlots, or by agri-business. It's an easy way to use your dollars to vote against the spread of toxins in our bodies, land, and water.

FIVE Use your buying power to encourage and support good behavior by private industries, which have very little incentive to improve their environmental practices. And use your political choices to support sensible government regulation of those industries.

SIX Along the same lines, support thoughtful innovations in manufacturing and production. Hint: Drilling for oil is no longer an innovation.

SEVEN Prioritize. Think hardest when buying large objects; don't fret too much over the small ones. The paper-bag puzzle is worth thinking about, but an energy-sucking refrigerator deserves more of your attention.

EIGHT Vote. Political engagement enables the spread of environmentally conscious policies. Without public action, thoughtful individuals are swimming upstream.

NINE Don't feel guilty. Bumming out leads to burning out and that doesn't get us anywhere.

TEN Enjoy what you have—the things that are yours alone, and the things that belong to none of us. Both are nice, but the latter are precious. Those things that we cannot manufacture and should never own—water, air, birds, trees—are the foundation of life's pleasures.

EVERYBODY'S WORKIN' FOR THE WEEKEND

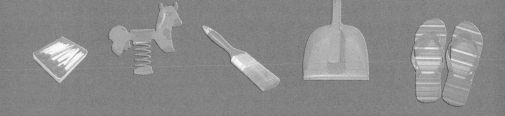

It is, in the immortal words of R. Kelly, the freakin' weekend. He's about to have him some fun—are you? Most of us view our weekends as sacrosanct—two days of blessedly uninterrupted time that we can use any way we see fit, whether that means working, playing, tidying, traveling, or just sitting quietly for a few moments of contemplation. (As if.) Whatever your plans may be, there are plenty of ways to go green.

PLAY'S THE THING

Remember the lesson *The Wizard of Oz* taught us: What you're looking for may be in your own backyard. Translation: No need to suffer flying monkeys or other travel hazards when there are plenty of kicks to be had out back—and in addition to avoiding wicked witches, you won't have any pesky eco-pangs about using jet or car fuel!

GRILL BIT

They always say the great American pastime is baseball or eating apple pie or something. Don't they? But these days it's another backyard tradition that gives those old standbys a run for their money: barbecuing. And firing up the grill is a fine way to get outside with friends and family to prepare a meal the history of which you can trace.

Before we get to the meat of this section, a little linguistic appetizer: the word barbecue apparently originated with the Taino Indians of Haiti, says the *Green Guide*—a consumer-focused newsletter and website (*www.thegreenguide.com*)—and was adopted (with relish!) by Bostonians in the early 1700s, spreading to Texas by the mid-1800s. We know you have questions about your grill, so now we present the FAQ on your BBQ.

AMERICA'S COMBINED FOURTH OF JULY COOK-OUTS CONSUME ENOUGH ENERGY TO MEET THE RESIDENTIAL DEMAND OF FLAGSTAFF, ARIZONA, FOR A YEAR.

Q. What kind of grill should I get?

A. You can choose from gas, electric, charcoal, or wood-burning. Of those options, gas is the most efficient—even more efficient than your regular stove—and burns more cleanly than wood and charcoal. Of course, it doesn't lend that yummy flavor to barbecue that makes it … well, barbecue. If you're keen on using wood, go for sustainably harvested hickory or mesquite. And keep an eye on the rise of corn grills, which burn dried kernels. Whatever you choose, know that charcoal is, for lack of a better word, gross. It can contain coal dust, limestone, and borax, among other things. On top of that, lighter fluid is as bad for you as you'd think from the smell. Would you cook lasagna just after spraying oven cleaner?

Q. What should I do with leftover ash?

A. Some gardens will thrive on wood ash, if you have the right soil type. You could ask a local garden center or plant person for advice. Sadly, charcoal gets another demerit in this department, as its ash is generally too toxic to reuse.

Q. Where's the best place to buy meat for the barbie?

A. Increasing numbers of ranchers are selling their products through farmers' markets, online mail-order sites, small natural-food stores, and farm stands, where they can build relationships with curious consumers—and bring in a little more cash than they do by selling to an industrial distributor.

Q. What about grilling soy-based products like tofu dogs and veggie burgers?

A. Here's the thing: some people choose not to eat meat because they're worried about the impacts it has on the planet. Raising, transporting, slaughtering, and packaging meat causes land, water, and air pollution—not to mention a pile of dead animals, which makes some people squeamish. The Union of Concerned Scientists says a quarter of the current threats to U.S. ecosystems and wildlife comes from meat and poultry production. Soy isn't a perfect solution—vast plantations are replacing Amazon rainforest, for one thing—but the American Journal of Clinical Nutrition says meat production takes more land (6 to 17 times as much), water (4.4 to 26 times), fossil fuels (6 to 20 times), and chemicals (6 times) than soy production. In fact, meat lost in every category. When processing and transport is factored in, the difference becomes less extreme, but it's still there. Meat-based diets use about twice as many environmental resources as soy-based diets. Despite concerns about deforestation and genetic engineering, soy appears to be the winner here.

Q. So, with that knowledge, should I give up grilling meat?

A. Let's be careful not to make the situation too black-and-white. There is some indication in these studies that sustainably raised, locally procured meat-based diets can hold their own, environmentally, against heavily processed, far-shipped veggie diets. So it's likely that eating local bacon is better than eating frozen veggie burgers from faraway lands—not just gastronomically but ecologically.

Dee-licious! Now what's for dessert?

The Astroturf Ain't the Only Thing That's Green

There have always been three primary reasons to love the Super Bowl: beer, commercials, and ass-slapping. But now there's a fourth reason, as the NFL planted native trees and bought renewable-energy certificates to offset greenhouse-gas emissions from Super Bowl XLI. Yes, fans, this could mean guilt-free beer farts! "Carbon mitigation: that to me is where the excitement, the challenge, and the opportunity are," said NFL Director of Environmental Programs Jack Groh (who might need to get out more). The Super Bowl has incorporated green elements for 14 years, but the 2007 game was the first to offset its emissions.

Such football-licious sustainability came hot on the heels of other sporting events that have gone for the green, including an ethanol-fueled Indy 500, climate-neutral soccer World Cup, and recycle-happy Turin Olympics. Which means Sundays on the couch just officially became activism. Sweet!

IT'S A FAMILY AFFAIR

The best thing about backyard noodling is that it's fun for all ages. Your yard can be a hands-on learning center for your kids. As an added bonus, the activities you do together not only create

If your weekends are eaten up by always ravenous home-improvement projects, take heart: fixing things yourselves (rather than buying a new replacement) is a great way to earn green stars. Additionally, in recent years fixer-upper options have taken on a greener sheen.

Consumers have tuned in to the benefits of eco-timber, sustainably harvested cork and bamboo flooring, and low-VOC paint, moving green home-building supplies out of the fringe and into the mainstream. "There's no question where this is going; it's hot," says Timothy Taylor. His company, Environmental Home Center (*www.environmentalhomecenter.com*), started in an 800-square-foot Seattle storefront in 1992; by 2006 it had become a multimillion-dollar business Taylor hopes to take nationwide.

Established national chains are also noticing the green tint in buyer preferences: Home Depot, for instance, has unveiled an "Eco Options" marketing theme that helps customers locate green(er) products. Eco-friendly can mean more expensive, but all involved have high hopes for economies of scale lowering prices. And remember, you don't always have to spend to make improvements: just making sure your dwelling is properly insulated can satisfy your home-improvement urges and make the place feel like new.

a bonding opportunity, they also mean more helping hands! (Hint: Teach toddlers to love weeding.)

> Plant a vegetable garden, checking in on it regularly and talking about the changes you see happening.

> Plant a native tree that your child can name and care for.

> Start a worm bin for some wriggly composting fun!

> Create habitat that will attract native critters; when they show up, learn about them together through field guides and observation.

> Eat meals outside when possible.

> Create an early appreciation for camping by pitching a tent in your own back yard or neighborhood.

> Don't have a yard? Even a city sapling or the phases of the moon can be good tools for talking about seasons, pollution, and other green themes.

BUGGER!

If your weekend or vacation plans include epidermal flaunting, you'll want to make sure your precious pores don't get bitten, burned, or otherwise abused.

You probably know that most conventional insect repellents contain DEET (also listed on labels as N, N-Diethyl-m-toluamide or N, N-Diethyl-3-Methyl benzamide). Mosquitoes most definitely dislike DEET, but unfortunately your eyes and skin also find it irritating. And in some drastic cases, DEET has been associated with lethargy, confusion, disorientation, and mood swings.

In addition to its immediate offenses, DEET is like a houseguest who never leaves. It breaks down very slowly, and is thus considered a persistent environmental contaminant. A recent U.S. Geological Survey report on water contaminants listed it as one of the compounds most frequently found in the nation's streams. The EPA regards DEET as "slightly toxic" to birds, fish, and aquatic invertebrates—which sounds akin to being "a little pregnant."

You can at least minimize exposure to DEET by using a product containing 10% or less, such as Off! Skintastic Family Formula or Cutter All Family. But if you want to do your bug-bite prevention au naturel, try these tactics:

› Wear long sleeves and long pants in light colors. (Some research shows that mosquitoes are more attracted to Goth outfits than golfer garb.)

› Bugs are worst at dawn and dusk, so bunker down at those hours.

› Stagnant water really puts mosquitoes in the mood, so inspect your property for potential larvae hot spots, such as plant trays, gutters, birdbaths, and puddles.

› Make sure your screens are actually screens (patch holes!).

Finally, here's the quick buzz on DEET-free insect repellents. Remember that while insect repellents made of botanical oils may not be as effective as DEET, frequent reapplication can help. (Your mantra: slather.) But be sure to test a small area of skin first, as some people are allergic to citrus or other aromatic plant oils. The following brands can be found at natural-food stores.

› Bite Blocker, which uses soybean oil as its active ingredient.

› Green Ban, a plant-based option that also claims to repel ticks.

› Buzz Away, an all-natural solution that comes in spray or towelette form, handy for travel.

REGARD THE YARD

While it may not be considered a particularly thrilling way to spend your weekend, yard work is, if nothing else, a time-honored tradition.

So Lawn, Farewell

Despite the fact that lawns made purely of mowable grass are downright unnatural, there are 40 million acres of lush lawn in the United States. Some 54 million people mow their lawns each week in the summer, using 800 million gallons of gas a year. In some cities, two-thirds of available fresh water goes on lawns, and more than 5% of urban air pollution comes from gas-powered lawn widgets. Seventy million pounds of pesticide get spewed on home lawns, trees, and shrubs a year, polluting groundwater and sending phosphates and nitrates into lakes and streams, where they generate algae blooms that choke other plant life. All so you can keep up with the Joneses! So quit it with the lawns. Embrace native species and a less manicured look, set up a system to catch rain for watering the garden or lawn, and tell the Joneses to mind their own business.

If it helps to up your excitement level, try thinking of yard work as a multi-event, backyard sport of sorts. A yard-a-thon, if you will. Now go for the green!

SUBURBAN LAWNS AND GARDENS USE HEAVIER PESTICIDE APPLICATIONS PER ACRE THAN AGRI-CULTURE.

WEED IT AND WEEP

Before you begin to rage against weeds, remember: a weed is simply a plant that is not desired in the place it's growing. Plants growing in compacted soil (common on housing sites) and in unnatural conditions are often un-healthy, and unhealthy plants are the first to be attacked by pests and weeds.

It's fairly well known that most commercial weed killers are a toxic blight to all things green. If you feel compelled to squirt something in a weed's face, try regular old white vinegar instead. However! The only tactic that will not disturb anything but weeds is ... weeding. Yes, it's best to stop those spawning plants in their tracks the old-fashioned way, with or without one of many newfangled tools like a standing dandelion puller or a flame-weeder. As your back aches and your brow sweats, take solace in knowing weeding is the technique used in the famous gardens of Versailles, Beijing's Summer Palace, and Monticello. So you're a part of herbicide-free history!

RAKISH CHARM

Ah, autumn. The brilliant hues, the sweet smells, the back-breaking hours of raking. Here's an idea: would raking seem less tedious if the results went

If you must mow, keep this comparison list handy and consider all your options.

> Gasoline Powered. One EPA estimate says using a gas mower for an hour pollutes as much as driving your car 20 miles, and others venture much higher guesses. Say you mow your lawn one hour per week, April through November. Even using the EPA's low-end number, you would need to cut at least 700 miles off your yearly driving to keep your family emissions level down to that of your pre-lawn life. And then there are your precious lungs to consider as you inhale a stew of particulates. If you're living green, gas mowers are a no-go.
> Electric Powered. At a cost of $190 to $500, plug-in models are limited by the length of their extension cord and will only work if your entire lawn is within reach of a power source. Also: they use electricity!
> Cordless Battery-Operated. These run about 60 to 90 minutes per charge and can go farther—but are pricier—than their tethered brethren.
> Manual Push Reels. Reel mowers offer a durable, effective, trash- and emissions-free (after manufacturing) choice. They are silent, fairly cheap ($80-$200), an excellent source of exercise, free to operate, emit nothing, and leave grass clippings to fertilize the lawn or have a handy catch-bag. For the reel deal, check out *www.reelmowerguide.com*.

beyond the yard waste bin? Because instead of bagging your leaves, you can actually make good use of them. Partially decomposed deciduous leaves are generally considered the world's best mulch, with a special name: leaf mold. Your trees will appreciate being mulched with their own leaves for the winter, and the rest of your plants won't complain either. You can rake piles of whole leaves around trunks, or run the (push) mower first to chop them into smaller pieces. (Chopping serves two purposes: the leaves will decompose more quickly, and the wind will blow them about less easily.) Plants of all sizes can use 2 to 3 inches of leafy mulch; just leave a couple of inches of open space around the base for air circulation. In the early spring, you'll see that the leaves on the bottom have decayed into succulent crumbs.

Or you could start a leaf-mold factory: find a place in your yard to pile all your deciduous leaves, soak them with water, and let them be for a couple of years. Maybe you want to make a wooden box for them, or put them in a commercial compost bin—whatever works with your yard's aesthetic. Just leave the leaves and come back to find a pile of humus that would cost you an arm and a leg anywhere else. Leaf mold, as mulch, is somewhat beyond compare—it is stable and has excellent moisture retention. Beneficial fungi play a major role in leaf decomposition, and it is clear that a fungi-rich soil is excellent for most garden plants and trees. The extra rotting time allows the leaves to decompose more completely and become more biologically stable than the insta-mulch option.

If you still can't abide keeping your leaves (and your city doesn't offer a yard-waste collection service), ask community gardens, schools, or composting businesses if they would like them. Whatever you do, please don't burn them. Burning your own yard waste is illegal in many states, and it also pollutes.

COMPOST-IT NOTES

So you say you want to join the ever-growing, ever-greening ranks of composters. First, we advise taking a look at the vast range of compost options available at a website like *www.composters.com*. Food composter choices run the gamut from a glorified bucket with holes to a hard plastic capsule on a spit. For example, you can buy a galvanized

Every Worm Is Sacred

Not for the faint of heart, but super-cool: Worm bins are fairly simple, highly efficient, and great for food waste. They require a bit of work at the beginning, plus ongoing maintenance of proper worm habitat. The product they yield—vermicompost—is considered the highest quality food-based compost. And if you have kids around, a worm bin is like a circus in a box.

Once you've got your receptacle ready to go—you could even build your own wooden bin and let the kids decorate it—soak dead leaves, shredded paper, and/or fine wood shavings in water, fill the bin with this material, and dump in the worms. (Not earthworms: red wiggler worms that you'll get from a friend with a worm bin or order from a worm business.) Start off slowly, feeding the worms a bucket of food scraps each week until the population expands enough to handle all your food scraps. Worms head up the decomposition team, but they are aided by other important decomposers in the bin: mites, fungus, sow bugs, caterpillars, slugs, and so forth.

trash can, drill small holes in it for drainage, and bury the bottom about a foot below ground. Simply throw food in it until it fills up, then neglect it for 10 months or so. Presto, change-o: compost.

You may be familiar with the concepts of "aerobic" and "anaerobic" decomposition. Aerobic makes a better end product, and compost bins in this category will either be worm domiciles or will involve some version of constantly turning the compost to integrate oxygen into the mix. Folding air in allows helpful organisms to thrive and chow down on organic waste, thereby converting it to compost. Anaerobic bins have their own benefits, most notably the absence of work. You won't have to turn your compost, but you'll get a far inferior result—and a stronger odor.

Choosing a compost system is ultimately a very personal decision, and one that depends on what you will try to compost and the amount of time you have to spend helping the compost along.

KEEP IT CLEAN, PEOPLE

When you arrive home from a long week of work (or disengage from the computer after a long day of telecommuting), chances are the way you'll want to spend your weekend is to do some eco-cleaning. Not so much? Well, perhaps knowing that you're cleaning green will at least make scrub-a-dub duty less irritating—to both you and the environment.

Want to rid your broom closet of toxic cleaners? Try making your own with four everyday ingredients: white vinegar, castile soap, baking soda, and water. Baking soda is the scrubber; vinegar is the sanitizer; soap is the ... soap (but don't mix it with the vinegar); and water is magic! Search the web for recipes, add a little elbow grease, and you'll be ready to hit the dirt.

IT'S A WASH

Winking bald men and giggling teddy bears would have you believe otherwise, but the cleaning products we've come to love and trust over the decades are not so friendly. In 2003, cleaning products were responsible for 10% of poison exposures reported to poison-control centers, half of them involving kids under age six. The chemicals in these products—many of which have not been tested by the EPA—can harm our health, affect our indoor air quality, and cause damage if they're disposed of improperly. But, hey, at least your toilet smells fresh.

Here's the dirt on some common products, and a few ideas for substitutes.

Washing dishes and laundry: Most mainstream detergents are made from petroleum and can contain hormone disruptors. Their strong fragrances can trigger asthma and allergic reactions.

Switch to: Fragrance-free products and plant-based cleaners made from corn, citrus, or coconut oil, and nonchlorine bleach.

Using antibacterial soaps and cleansers: Our obsession with ridding ourselves of bacteria is leading to—wait for it—the growth of more resistant bacteria.
Switch to: Good old-fashioned hand washing with regular old soap. It's worked for millennia!

Making your glass and tile sparkle: These cleaners often contain bleach, which can burn skin and eyes and be fatal if swallowed. Oh, and its manufacture creates dioxins.
Switch to: White vinegar mixed with water for bathroom and

kitchen surfaces and windows, and hot, soapy water for surfaces that have touched raw meat or eggs.

Cleaning drains, ovens, and toilet bowls: Ranking right up there as the most dangerous cleaning products, items from this powerful trio contain bleach, lye, and other potent stuff.

Get Your Ash in Gear

Ever wondered what baking soda is, where it comes from, and why we can use it for everything from teeth to cakes to bathtubs? Prepare to be astounded.

Baking soda is sodium bicarbonate, a naturally occurring crystalline compound that comes from Green River, Wyoming. Turns out Wyoming holds the world's largest reserves of trona, otherwise known as sodium sesquicarbonate—a key ingredient in this household staple. An estimated 100 billion tons or more sit right under the high-steppe desert. Almost all baking soda made in the United States hails from there, and a quarter of the world's supply does too.

As for its cleaning properties, we can chalk that up to the magic of crystal alkalinity. Chemically basic baking soda neutralizes the acids in grease, dirt, and other messes and stinks. It's also a crystal, so it scrubs, but is soft and dissolves in water, so it doesn't scratch. It's amply present in our environment and our bodies to begin with, and appears to be nontoxic (although it should be kept away from the little ones). We use it for leavening and eat it. So basically, it's yummier dirt.

Switch to: Use a drain snake or enzyme-based products to unclog drains. Clean ovens with an overnight application of water and baking soda paste. For toilets, pour one cup of borax in at night, then scrub and flush the next morning.

Polishing furniture and metals: Corrosive and irritating to eyes and lungs, these gems are often made with petroleum and formaldehyde.
Switch to: For furniture, polish with a one-to-one mix of olive oil and vinegar. Rub copper with vinegar with a little salt dissolved in it; rub silver with toothpaste; rub brass with a paste made of equal parts vinegar and flour, plus a small bit of salt.

Freshening the air: Some people love the sensation of Mountain Mist and Spring Lilac searing their nostrils and lungs, but others say the chemical fragrances are dangerous.
Switch to: Baking soda, the world's best odor-eater, or products scented with essential plant oils. Or, for a completely radical notion: fresh air! We hear it works wonders.

KEEN, GREEN CLEANING MACHINES

The word *chores* rhymes with *bores* and *snores*—coincidence? We think not. But while scientists don't seem to be making any progress toward those robot maids we saw in *The Jetsons*, we do have a few trusty machines available to assist with our drudgery. The question for the green cleaner, however, is whether said machines are to be adored or deplored.

One way to ensure you're buying an energy-efficient home appliance is by cross-referencing the *Consumer Reports* recommendations with handy Energy Star ratings. Energy Star is a labeling project of the EPA; when you go into an appliance store these days, any appliance with an Energy Star rating should have a flier inside describing its energy use. March into the appliance store with a *Consumer Reports* ranking, a budget, and knowledge of your machine needs (height, capacity, decorative touches), then compare the Energy Star details of the machines that could fit your bill.

More expensive? Typically, yes. Worth it? Absolutely. In the *Consumer Guide to Home Energy Savings*, the ACEEE estimates that a new appliance may save you up to $100 a year in water and/or electricity bills, and your utility may also offer a rebate. Keeping the long-term payback in mind as you shop will help with any sticker shock.

DISHING IT OUT

Perhaps by now you've heard the dish on dishwashers. If fully loaded but not overloaded, if no prerinsing is done, if low-energy cycles are used, then yes! A dishwasher is more water-efficient and hygienic than doing dishes the old-fashioned way.

The average dishwasher uses about 15 gallons of water per load, while the average dish-washer (that would be you) uses about 5 gallons of water per minute at the sink. If you have just a few dirty dishes, you can minimize waste by stopping up the drain or filling a basin instead of keeping the water running. On the other hand, if you space out at the sink with the tap going full blast and

Washed Up

> 400—loads of laundry washed by a typical U.S. household in one year
> 35 billion—loads of laundry washed every year in the United States
> 73—percentage of U.S. households with washers and dryers
> 7—percentage of washing machines replaced by U.S. consumers each year
> 76,000—annual electricity consumption, in gigawatt hours, of U.S. washers and dryers
> 38 to 58—percentage reduction in energy use by high-efficiency washing machines compared to conventional washers
> 40—gallons of water used per full load of clothing in a conventional washer
> 18 to 25—gallons of water used per full load of clothing in a washer certified by Energy Star, an EPA and U.S. Department of Energy program
> 16,000—annual gallons of water used for clothes washing by a typical American household
> 7,000—gallons of water saved annually by using an Energy Star washing machine
> 13 million—annual metric tons of greenhouse gas emissions from washers and dryers in the United States
> 12—average capacity, in pounds of clothes, of both high-efficiency washing machines and traditional washers
> 140,204—largest quantity of laundry, in pounds, ever washed in a nine-hour working day (by staff at Central Linen Service in Kilkenny, South Australia, May 18, 1989)

start thinking about how much you love the plates with the blue stripe on them, and how annoyed you still are that your brother ended up with more of them than you—well, your dreams of being green have gone down the drain.

It's worth it to spend the time and money to get a dishwasher that works. You won't need to waste faucet water on prerinsing, or money on repairs.

SPIN CYCLE

Unless you spend your life in a plastic playsuit (not recommended!), you're going to need more than a sponge-off to get your clothes clean. But from washing to drying, keeping your duds spiffy is a major energy and water suck. Fortunately, there are ways to make washing day more efficient.

Foremost, you'll need the right machine for the job. Top-loading, vertical-axis washers are basically an automated washtub, filling with water to wet all the clothing and swishing it about in detergent. Front-loading, horizontal-axis types partially fill with water and whip the clothes through, like a mill wheel in a stream. They're actually gentler on fabrics, quieter, and use far less detergent.

An older top-loading washer probably uses about 40 gallons of water per load. New, efficient machines—mainly front-loading, but some top-loading—use 16 to 25 gallons per load. Less water means less energy to heat the water, and that's the main drain with washers; up to 90% of the energy they use goes toward heating. Fronties can also spin faster and extract extra moisture, shortening time in the energy-sucking dryer.

In sum, buying a new, efficient washer means lower water and water-heater use; less generated sewage; consumer support of energy-efficient technologies;

cleaner, longer-lasting garments; and inspiring similar behaviors in others. Your personal energy impact will be improved in every way. If you decide to buy, look for the Energy Star rating. And pledge to pass your still-good washer on to someone who needs it, rather than send it to the landfill!

If you'd have to launder money to afford such an upgrade right now, never fear: simply wash in cold water, and see how the savings add up.

THE FIRST AMERICAN PATENT FOR A CLOTHESPIN WAS ISSUED IN 1832.

HANG TOUGH

Wondering about the energy-sucking effects of going for a tumble? Get this: the EPA doesn't even give Energy Star ratings to dryers, because they all use about the same amount of energy. Which is to say, a lot. It's actually something like 800 kilowatt-hours a year, second only to the fridge on the list of home-appliance energy hogs.

So clotheslines, drying racks, and the like are the best eco-options. Or try a combination: getting your clothes partway dry in the dryer and then hanging them up to dry the rest of the way can reduce static cling while simultaneously decreasing both the energy used during drying and the necessary hang-drying time.

Speaking of static: Your home will be a happier, healthier place if no fabric softener darkens your dryer. Both liquid and sheets contain a stunning amount of notoriously toxic chemicals. Individually, some of these chemicals have been linked to cancer, and it's not likely they've been studied much in combination.

A less-toxic solution is to add our friend baking soda during the rinse cycle or white vinegar during the wash cycle (but don't use vinegar if you're also using bleach, another toxic favorite). If dousing your clothes in vinegar sounds like too much of a stretch from your current routine, there are much-less-scary natural varieties of fabric softener widely available. Try Seventh Generation, for starters.

GETTING TAKEN TO THE CLEANERS

Under EPA regulations, dry cleaners in residential buildings must phase out the toxic solvent perchloroethylene by the year 2020. "Perc," an air pollutant and probable carcinogen, has been linked to cancer, neurological damage, reduced sperm count, nausea, and miscarriages. One study of people living above a dry cleaner in New York found elevated levels of perc in their blood, urine, and breast milk, as well as vision impairment. About 28,000 dry cleaners use perc, but only 1,300 of them will be affected by the new ruling.

As old machines wear out, dry cleaners must replace them with non-perc machines. The EPA rules also require nonresidential dry cleaners to install devices to detect solvent leaks and take steps to reduce emissions. Health risks to nearby residents may be "significantly higher than EPA considers acceptable in some buildings until the phaseout … is complete," according to the fact sheet accompanying the rules. But only for a few more years!

If 2020 sounds like a long way away, another hope is the new professional clothes-washing trend, "wet cleaning." Cleaning businesses purchase computer-controlled fabric-washing equipment that features four extract speeds, air bubble power, 89 user-defined programs, residual moisture control sensors … and that's only the beginning. Wet cleaning is environmentally preferable to dry cleaning since it avoids the laundry list of problems associated with perchloroethylene.

Another avoidance mechanism: get rid of fabrics that require dry cleaning, or try hand-washing them (carefully). If your fancy work clothes render that an impossible option, at least urge your cleaning establishment to transition to wet-cleaning.

WE GOTTA GET OUT OF THIS PLACE

Tahiti … Copenhagen … East Hoboken … We're betting you spend at least some percentage of your working hours dreaming of how you can escape the daily routine. If you're trying to live, work, and play green, however, an attempt to square environmental sensibilities with wanderlust can bring on a serious case of wander paralysis. To limber up for those far-flung adventures, evaluate multiple modes of transport, and educate yourself on "carbon offsets."

AND YOU THOUGHT SNAKES ON A PLANE WERE TROUBLING

Vacations are supposed to leave you feeling relaxed, happy, and healthy—but if you travel by air, you might return home feeling worse than you did when you left.

Lonnie Thompson has clocked more hours above 18,000 feet than any other person in history, yet he doesn't exactly like climbing mountains. A masochist? No, just a hard-driving climate scientist.

Thompson treks up the highest peaks of the tropics—including the Himalayas and Andes—to extract ice-core samples. He then takes the samples back to giant refrigerated vaults at Ohio State University's Byrd Polar Research Center, where he analyzes the air and debris captured in the ice to get a picture of historic temperatures, greenhouse-gas levels, and weather events stretching back as many as 750,000 years.

"I think it's safe to say that worldwide, the warming trends of today are more dramatic than they have been in at least 5,000 years," Thompson says, adding that we've yet to really map how historical trends fit together. He's particularly worried about warming because his glacial stomping grounds are shrinking so fast they could vanish completely by mid-century, taking with them an invaluable geological archive.

Thompson—who says a typical day of drilling at 23,500 feet includes waking up in a snowed-in tent, digging out, eating breakfast in a kitchen carved out of snow, then spending the hours until sundown in a geodesic dome with a solar-powered drill collecting ice cores—once had a close call on a climb and doesn't climb for fun. "If I could get the necessary data by another, safer approach, I would," he says. "I believe the scientific and social importance of the data outweigh the risks."

All Hail the Rail

Travelers in the United States take 56% of our long-distance trip miles in a personal vehicle. Guess how much we travel long-distance by train? One percent. Yet according to the Union of Concerned Scientists, the train is miles better. In terms of impact on global warming, air pollution, water pollution, and habitat alteration, U.S. trains definitely come out ahead of planes and cars, with better ratings in all subcategories except common air pollution and land use.

One person who's tracking the untapped potential of trains is British entrepreneur Richard Branson, owner of the Virgin Group, which includes Virgin Records and Virgin Airlines. "Do we really need airplanes on short-haul routes where people could be traveling by train?" the mogul has pondered. "Personally, I think the answer is no. If we've got an adequate train service, people should be going by train, which produces about eight times less CO_2 than planes. If there's an adequate train service, I think it should be government mandated." And this from an airline exec? Jolly good.

Flying should not generally be the transportation option of choice for the environmentally minded, given its intensive use of resources (see sidebar, page 120). Besides the gazillions of gallons of jet fuel planes use, the emissions they spew, and the inefficiency of their engines—intercity buses consume less than one-fifth the energy jets do to cover the same distance—there's all that wasted snack mix. (Who speaks for the bagel chips?) Some airlines are waking up to the realities of climate change. British Airways, for one, offers passengers the chance to offset the emissions from their flights, but that method is controversial. And not only is jetsetting lousy for the Earth, it can harm your health: some countries require planes to be "disinsected," meaning the cabin is sprayed with pesticides. In short, airlines have a long way to go.

CRUISIN' FOR A BRUISIN'

While boat travel might seem another logical (if slow-going) solution to the flight-or-sit-tight conundrum, consider the following: The environmental

Fit to be Tied

We were just in the kitchen with Dinah, choo-ing over this factoid: nearly a billion wooden railroad ties hold together the railroads and subways of the United States. That's a lot of wood, and thus a lot of trees. It's also a lot of creosote, a preservative chemical used on wood and deemed by the EPA "probably a human carcinogen." The cost of wood, coupled with insurance against creosote-related litigation, is inspiring some rail operators to switch to ties made from recycled plastics and rubber—milk jugs, plastic bags, polystyrene cups, and so forth. Manufacturers claim that plastic ties are environmentally friendly, and that they last longer and resist humidity better than their wood counterparts. Makers of plastic ties now have less than 1% of the market, but they anticipate a growing share in years to come.

Ten Reasons You're Flying Unfriendly Skies

Remember when planes were the glamorous way to go? Neither do we, but we've heard tell. Now it seems it's all the airlines can do to throw a minuscule pack of pretzels our way and shame us for the size of our carry-on bags. What's worse, the air industry is responsible for spewing cargo loads of crud into our skies. Get a load of these sky-high stats:

> 87,000—number of flights completed in the United States each day, including commercial, private, and military
> 10—approximate number of gallons of crude oil required to make one gallon of jet fuel
> 11— percentage of total global, transportation-related carbon dioxide emissions released by airplanes
> 840 to 1,660 —pounds of carbon dioxide per passenger generated by a New York-to-Denver flight, about the same as an SUV generates in a month
> 53 million—gallons of jet fuel used per day by the U.S. airline industry
> 9,000—gallons of fuel for one Boeing 767 flight from New York to Los Angeles
> 1,712—percent increase in gallons of jet fuel used between 1965 and 2005
> 87—percent increase in commercial jet travel between 1985 and 2005
> 56—projected percent increase in airline travel between 2007 and 2020

problems in the cruise industry are staggering. Cruise ships are floating cities, with all of a regular city's emissions, solid and liquid waste, and public health problems, but little account-ability. Everything generated on the ship, from cocktail napkins to dry-cleaning fluids, has to go somewhere—and we all remember how much easier it was to pee in the pool than get out and go to the bathroom. Royal Caribbean Cruises settled with the feds a few years back for, among other violations, rigging a tube that would completely bypass the pollution control system. That's right: They *had* a system, and then they developed another system to avoid it. Think long and hard before you sign up for a shipload of fun.

YOU CAN GO YOUR OWN WAY

Say you're a conscientious green, but it's your wedding anniversary, and you think the planet can splurge on you for once. You're taking a plane, dammit,

Don't Worry, It's a Rental

An environmentally focused rental group, EV Rental Cars, has joined forces with a big-name rental company, Budget, to offer hybrid choices in select metropolitan areas in California, Arizona, and Nevada. Rumor has it hybrids will join other fleets in farther-flung markets in the future, so keep the hope alive. Each time you must rent a car, search the web and, if you find no hybrids available, be sure to mention your disappointment to the rental agent.

and you're staying in water-hogging, energy-snarfing hotels. But you still feel a little twinge. So how can you travel with the least impact?

Let's pretend you're headed to Italy. First, consider stocking up on carbon offsets to counter the miles you'll be flying (see sidebar for more info). Alternatively, you could simply donate what you judge to be the correct amount of cash to the environmental group of your choice.

In recent years, a product called "carbon offsets" has sprung up to help everyone from world travelers to wedding guests feel better about their impact. How does it work? You calculate the dollar value of the greenhouse gases your life (or particular event) produces, and then spend that amount on offsets sold by one of the many groups now in the biz. Your investment ideally goes toward renewable energy or sustainable development projects. You feel better, and the project managers feel richer. A win-win, right? Not so fast.

Increasingly, critics of offsets point out the obvious: you're still emitting big, bad clouds of carbon, and the only thing that will really help the climate is for you to cut that out. (Our favorite spot-on parody is a British website called Cheat Neutral that "offsets" adultery by paying someone else to be faithful.) Offset providers maintain that every dollar spent is a dollar that wouldn't otherwise be supporting renewable energy, and say it's an effective solution.

If you do decide to buy, do your research, and know that to be considered legit, offset businesses should be certified by an independent third party.

Offset We Go,
Into the Wild
Blue Yonder

Once you get to Italy, use public transportation. Do not rent a car, do not rent a motorized scooter, do not fly within the country. Plan your trip using buses, trains, ferries, bicycles, and your feet. This may raise a fear that you will not "see Italy"—that is, that you will not be able to check off ten famous sites during your ten days. But what would we say to two people touring Vermont who felt the need to drive to a new quaint town every day? Their frantic pace would eliminate relaxation and the possibility of spontaneous experience, as well as any aspect of authentic Vermont life.

AMERICAN WORKERS LEFT 421 MILLION VACATION DAYS UNUSED IN 2005. HEY, WE'LL TAKE 'EM!

Whether your destination is as big as a boot or smaller than a breadbox, wherever you go, the key is to pick an area that contains several of your interests in proximity. In Italy, let's say a few historic palazzos, an art museum, an excellent restaurant (or two, or three—molte bene!). Another idea would be to do an online search for "eco-vacation" or "ecotourism" or "eco-holiday" in Italy or other countries you're interested in, and see what turns up. There are plenty of ecotourism resources online—after all, they don't call it the World Wide Web for nothing.

COLD DAY AT THE BEACH

We've all been trained to slather on the sunscreen, but what happens when said sunscreen poses problems of its own?

Sunscreens can contain chemicals associated with skin irritation and rashes, and some contain suspected carcinogens. (Always avoid using sunscreens on children younger than six months, unless there is no other way to protect them from the sun.) These chemicals can be bad for you and for the environment, washing off of your body when you swim and messing with underwater animals and plants. Try these other methods instead:

› Organic sunblocks. Many of those green cosmetic companies noted back in Chapter 1, "You're Soaking in It," make them, including Jason, Avalon, and Aubrey.

› Hemp-based sunblock. Harking back to the aforementioned miracles of hemp, some companies, including Burt's Bees and the U.K.-based Yaoh (*www.yaoh. co.uk*), make natural sunblock using hemp seed oil.

› Umbrellas and parasols, wide-brimmed hats, and clothes that cover your skin are all good ways to say nay to rays.

› Sunglasses with UV protection. Your eyes will thank you.

Weekend Grist in Five Seconds or Less

The most effective way to clean the bathroom is:

A. Shower it with chemicals
B. Scrub-a-dub-dub with vinegar and baking soda
C. Total remodel
D. Um, I'm pretty sure it cleans itself?

If you answered B, call it good and spend the weekend outside.

ON AN
EVENING KEEL

It may be dark outside, but the sun never sets on environ-mental concerns! It's likely that you have more control over greening your after-work or at-home activities anyway, so it's the perfect time to make the choices that can make a difference. As you might suspect, we have a few suggestions for ending the day with green in mind, whether your nightlife involves staying in, heading out, or getting down.

GREEN: IT'S WHAT'S FOR DINNER

What's first on the evening agenda? Dinner! Which provides the perfect opportunity to present six philosophical dilemmas that have plagued thinkers through
the ages: Paper or plastic? Why is organic so expensive? Should I eat locally?
Should I be a vegetarian? Did my seafood have a happy childhood? And finally,
one that Socrates was said to have struggled with for years: Are genetically
modified organisms invading my diet?

EVERYTHING YOU ALWAYS WANTED TO KNOW ABOUT SACKS (*BUT WEREN'T AFRAID TO ASK)

What seems like an innocent trip to the grocery store to pick up dinner can present some of our most harrowing conservation questions. First and foremost, of
course, is the legendary "paper or plastic" conundrum.

The answer (drumroll, please)? Neither. While the quantifiable difference
between paper and plastic bags is minimal, the best option is to bring your
own bag.

It is generally understood that the plastic bag production process generates less water pollution, less air pollution, and less solid
waste than paper. Making something out of plastic just seems to
be easier than making something out of wood, which goes a long
way toward explaining why we have so much plastic packaging
today: It's cheap. In addition, and you can bet the plastic industry
is cackling over this, the bags take up less space in landfills.

In early 2007, San Francisco became the first city in the United States to ban plastic bags, following the lead of South Africa, Bangladesh, Paris, and other places that have sacked the popular sacks. Ireland levies a tax on the ubiquitous baggies, and Swedish mega-retailer IKEA recently instituted a five-cent charge for each plastic bag it doles out.

As to which manufacturing process uses less energy, they may be equal. It depends in part on whether you calculate two plastic bags for each paper bag, because store clerks frequently double-bag when using plastic. Comparative Environmentalism 101 is tough!

Of course, paper bags trump plastic in the renewable resource realm, being made from trees rather than oil or gas, and being more commonly accepted by community recycling programs. Also, paper bags are biodegradable and far less likely to disturb natural ecosystems in the manner of plastic bags, which have a nasty tendency to be mistaken for jellyfish and wind up doing bad things to the innards of turtles—to cite just one example.

But sometimes the bag dilemma can distract us from bigger issues. Picture this scenario: You're driving down the street and your eye is caught by a plastic bag snared in a tree. "Gross!" you think, "Some jerk has been littering again! Those plastic bags are a wasteful, American consumerist eyesore! Turtles are going to die!" Guess what? That flapping plastic bag is a distraction from the much more

Having dinner at a restaurant doesn't mean compromising on your green eating goals. Just ask and ye shall receive the scoop on what's being brought to your table. Here are five questions for the waiter, manager, or owner at your favorite bistro.

> Do you use ingredients from a local farm or producer?
> Do you use organic ingredients?
> Is your meat free of antibiotics and hormones? How is it raised?
> Is your seafood sustainably farmed? Where does it come from?
> Do you compost leftovers or donate them to community organizations?

For more suggestions on approaching farmers, grocery stores, and restaurants, see *www.sustainabletable.com*.

important, all-too-often overlooked fact that you are driving—driving a particulate-spewing, gas-devouring, pavement-loving machine.

In the end, the most important choices you can make in terms of air and water pollution, global climate change, and ecosystem destruction are those that relate to transportation, household efficiency, and food consumption.

But in the meantime, bring your own bag.

ACHIEVING THE BIG O: WHY IS ORGANIC FOOD SO PRICEY?

Eating organic is generally considered a good way to avoid a side order of scary pesticides with your meals. So why do stores make organic food so prohibitively expensive?

In part it's because organic agriculture, by and large, does not receive the same amount of governmental support as conventional agriculture. Organic food accounts for about 2.5% of total food sales in the United States. Many organic farms are too small to participate in government programs aimed at huge operations, and their diverse crops don't qualify for support aimed at monolithic crops.

In addition, inherent aspects of organic farming are simply expensive: the costs of labor, fertilizer, pest management, seeds, and baby animals are in most cases higher than for conventional products. Imagine the difference between pouring gallons of liquid into industrial irrigation pipes, versus laying, spreading, and blending in literally tons of compost using human labor. Which sounds cheaper and less labor-intensive to you?

Add to these the laws of capitalism—wholesalers, distributors, and grocery stores know that people will pay more for the organic label—and you've got yourself a high price for health.

THINK GLOBAL, EAT LOCAL

A growing movement is encouraging people to eat foods that are grown and produced within a 100-mile radius of where they live. Self-proclaimed "locavores" argue that eating local foods is even more important than eating organic, since in our global economy, it's estimated that food travels approximately 1,500 miles before landing on our plates. All that transportation trans-

Take a Bite Out of Chemicals

One way to offset some of the high cost of organics is to limit your spending to the produce most likely to be saturated in pesticides. Check out the Environmental Working Group's website (*www.foodnews.org*) to view a handy list ranking nonorganic produce by pesticide load. Here are the top ten most pesticide-laden fruits and veggies (from worst to ... somewhat less worst, but still alarming):

1. Peaches
2. Apples
3. Sweet bell peppers
4. Celery
5. Nectarines
6. Strawberries
7. Cherries
8. Pears
9. Grapes (imported)
10. Spinach

132   ON AN EVENING KEEL

lates into a long list of environmental evils, including the fuel, packaging, and energy required, plus the edging out of small, local farms. While the USDA "organic" sticker insures us against chemicals, it does not address farm size, shipping distances, fair prices for farmers or fair wages for workers, and has nothing to say about local economies. Although it addresses some of agriculture's most grievous, polluting trends, organic does nothing, per se, to address the corporatization of agriculture.

NEARLY 20% OF HUMAN-CAUSED GREENHOUSE-GAS EMISSIONS COMES FROM THE LIVESTOCK INDUSTRY—YES, INCLUDING COW FARTS.

Local farms cut down on the environmental toll of transport. Also, concerned eaters can visit local farms or talk with the growers to learn firsthand how your food is grown or raised. Smaller farmers are looking for a way to make more money per pound of produce; for the little guy, selling to a giant conglomerate doesn't pay. Direct access to local consumers means more profit, which is further enhanced by labeling and marketing products in a way that emphasizes conservation practices and all the effort and care put into raising vegetables or animals.

So are local foods always the answer? Certainly not for people whose 100-mile radius doesn't include a single farmers' market. If you have no other way of learning about how the food you're purchasing was grown or raised, the organic label is your only general guarantee of basic sustainability on the farm. Organic certification doesn't guarantee feedlot-free meat, for instance, but buying organic is better than buying blind. When feasible, however, locally produced foods are inherently fresher, tastier, and better for your health (not to mention the health of your local economy) than those that have stacked up frequent flier miles.

WHAT'S VEGETARIANISM GOT TO DO, GOT TO DO WITH IT?

Why do people commit to a vegetarian or vegan diet? Reasons vary widely, of course, but green worries often play a big part.

With pasture animals of all sorts, soil erosion and overgrazing are major environmental concerns. Disease can spread rapidly through crowded conditions,

Be a Hunter–Gatherer

Explore these websites for more information about where your food comes from and how much energy it takes to get to your belly.

> 100-Mile Diet, *www.100milediet.org*
> American Livestock Breeds Conservancy, *www.albc-usa.org*
> Chefs Collaborative, *www.chefscollaborative.org*
> Community Supported Agriculture, *www.localharvest.org/csa*
> FoodRoutes Network, *www.FoodRoutes.org*
> Locavores, *www.locavores.com*
> Renewing America's Food Traditions, *www.slowfoodusa.org/raft*
> Seed Savers Exchange, *www.seedsavers.org*
> Slow Food USA, *www.slowfoodusa.org*

leading to cycles of illness and medication. Feedlot conditions can exacerbate these problems. We address some meaty questions in the grilling section, but here are a few more fleshy facts to consider:

› Almost all meat birds today are Cornish Cross broilers, a hybrid chicken bred for rapid weight gain, efficient feed conversion, ease of plucking, uniformity of growth, and machine processing. The "free-range" label is misleading because it only requires that farms allow birds access to the outside. Cornish Cross reach market weight in six or seven weeks; at this point they are too heavy for their legs and sometimes cannot even walk to whatever range is available.

› Turkeys have been bred for superior breast meat for so long that they now literally have trouble standing upright, resulting in birds with lame, infected legs that can barely walk, let alone fly. Because these overbred turkeys aren't genetically diverse, they are vulnerable to disease and can only reproduce via artificial insemination. They're pumped full of antibiotics and fed not nuts, grains, and grass—their normal diet—but high-protein food, including slaughterhouse leftovers.

› Most pigs are raised in "concentrated animal feeding operations" (CAFOs), where they spend their lives being treated as protein on the hoof. With as many as 10,000 pigs per facility, each CAFO can produce as much waste as a town of 25,000 people. The waste is captured in ponds where heavy rainfalls, flooding, and poor sealing can result in overflows that poison local water tables.

› Feedlots crowd cattle ankle-deep in manure and urine, providing ideal conditions for the spread of pathogens like salmonella, listeria, and E. coli. We have seen massive beef and poultry recalls in the United States. Yet the industry's

solution—combating illness through antibiotic-laced feed—promotes danger-
ously disease-resistant strains of bacteria.

The moral of this sordid story: If you are going to eat meat, know the produc-
er, and try to make sure the flesh you favor is locally raised, organically certified,
and cruelty-free. And don't think you have to convert to some sort of tofu-
kumquat diet; even forgoing meat once or twice a week can make a difference.

BALANCING THE SCALES

If the horrors of the beef and poultry industries have you hurling yourself into
the sea, you might consider fish as another option. Indeed, fish can be a healthy
source of protein and other goodness, but as you might have guessed, you
should be mindful of whence your waterborne meal splashes forth.

Most of our animal-based foods were domesticated years ago, but fish still
roam wild in the depths of the oceans, doing their best to escape our clutches.
It's getting toward the last stand for far too many fish species, however, and the
issues for pescavores are complex and baffling.

To briefly summarize the negative side of fish consumption: First, overly
broad catch tools such as giant trawling nets can result in a large "bycatch" of
unwanted sea critters that perish prematurely. In some shrimp-trawling fisheries, for example, each pound of shrimp may come in with four to ten pounds of
bycatch. Don't buy fish caught by trawling.

Second, increased consumer demand, combined
with shrinking fish populations, has driven intense
depletion of stocks from fishing grounds—to the
point where populations cannot rebound. This is

Fish Tips

Still feel at sea? Here are some suggestions for avoiding suspicious fishes:

> In general, avoid fish that come from trawling, fish farming, and Atlantic fish runs
> Educate yourself about the fish you particularly like to buy, starting at Environmental Defense's webpage of fish links (*www.oceansalive.org*), where you'll find enough info to make you an expert, or at least a better shopper.
> Download a wallet-sized fish-advisory card from the Audubon Society or Environmental Defense. It's a handy reminder when shopping or supping that some species should be left alone.
> Finally, do not underestimate your own influence as a customer, whether in fine dining establishments or fish markets. If your waiter or fishmonger can't answer your questions, say you'll be shopping where you can buy from informed professionals.

called *overfishing*. If fish aren't given an opportunity to grow up and get it on, there won't be any new baby fish. It's simple, and fisherpeople are far from stupid, but economic desperation has driven several U.S. fisheries to collapse, the Atlantic cod being a tragic example. Don't buy from overfished areas.

Third, some fish farming has very bad implications for disease, genetic strength, and water pollution. Picture the dead zone under a salmon farm, where piles of fish poop (the remains of antibiotic-laden food) have smothered all signs of life. Catfish and shellfish farming, however, is well contained and has fewer impacts on water quality and wild strains. Friends don't let friends buy farmed salmon. Buy farmed clams instead.

Finally, on the consumer end, pollution in our waterways can result in fish laden with DDT, PCBs, dioxins, mercury, and their fellow poisons. These carcinogens and neurotoxins, which accumulate in fish flesh, are particularly threatening to developing fetuses and young children. The EPA maintains a database of fish-consumption advisories issued by state, tribal, and federal governments; check them out or call your state fish and wildlife department if you are concerned about the level of pollution in your local waterways.

Fortunately, as fish consumption has increased, these problems have spawned an ocean of concern from scientists, consumers, and fishermen. Together, they have created sustainably managed fisheries around the world that have kept fish, jobs, and cash plentiful.

GMOS: NO-NO OR GO-GO?

If you're tuned in to current environmental debates, you've likely heard the phrase "genetically modified organisms" (or GMOs). They sound like the stuff of mad scientists, and the truth about GMOs can be difficult to decipher, especially since different businesses define GMOs differently. One thing is certain: the field is rife with dogma. Companies that genetically modify food crops claim safety, environmental and consumer groups claim alarm, scientists argue, food-safety agencies procrastinate, and consumers—well, we're just trying to sort it all out.

Certainly, forcing hybrids that would never occur outside a test tube seems unnatural, but is it cause for alarm? We don't know. The potential for errors with genetic modification is sobering—the GMO industry has engineered crops to be pesticide-resistant, to have long shelf lives, to incubate pharmaceuticals

If You Like GMOs, You Might Also Like ...

Sci-fi and horror fans have rarely met a genetically modified organism they didn't like, as evidenced by the numerous movie plots featuring the spawn of scientific splicing and dicing. Here's a short list of GMOs to add to your DVD diet, if you dare:

> *The Island of Dr. Moreau* (1977, remade in 1996)
  This is not your father's *Fantasy Island*.
> *The Fly* (1958, remade in 1986)
  You're gonna need a bigger swatter.
> *Replicant* (2001)
  Plenty more where this came from.
> *The Alligator People* (1959)
  Prepare to flush!
> *DinoCroc* (2004)
  A toothy twofer.
> *Mansquito* (2005)
  'Nuf said.

("pharm crops"), and to achieve industrial pollutant remediation. The potential health harms of such crops include inadvertent allergenicity, development of antibiotic-resistant diseases, and the unintentional mixing of pharm crops with food crops. Environmental harms could include the invasion of nonmodified fields and the creation of superpests and superweeds.

It's highly likely that you'll pick up a few GMOs on your trip to the grocery store, since many processed foods contain corn or soybean—both of which are crops popular with the GMO set. As of 2004, for instance, 85% of the U.S. soy crop was genetically modified, accounting for some 63.6 million acres of soybeans. Statistics for 2003 indicate that at least 55% of soy worldwide is now genetically modified.

At this point in time, you have no way of knowing whether eating genetically modified soy, corn, and the like will harm you. Opponents of GMOs are requesting independent, scientifically rigorous testing of each modified crop and that GMO products be labeled so consumers at least have the option of avoiding modified crops.

The last major advance in agriculture was the advent of synthetic chemicals, seen as a twentieth-century miracle for farmers struggling to maintain productivity and fight pests. DDT was once considered a godsend—and it's now one of legions of chemicals outlawed in the United States. Should our government agencies ineptly bumble their way through regulating this latest revolution in agriculture, at our expense? For answers (and more questions) search the Internet for the Center for Food Safety, the True Food Network, and the Campaign to Label Genetically Engineered Foods.

MMM, LEFTOVERS

Once you've spent the time and money selecting locally grown, organic, pesticide-free, GMO-less ingredients for your dinner, you'll likely want to save every scrap of the leftovers. So how best to store your precious vittles? Choose glass containers instead of plastic if you can, and avoid polystyrene for long-term storage. Plates, dishtowels, or tinfoil make useful substitutes for plastic lids.

Okay. But what about the dinner scraps that aren't going into tomorrow's lunch? Home composting is the best choice. It keeps trash out of the waste stream, uses no chemicals, and enriches garden soil. Alas, composting is not always possible if those scraps include butter, free-range bacon bits, or other animal products. So then the question is, down the garbage disposal or into the trash? In landfills, peels, rinds, and cores have no access to oxygen and hence biodegrade very slowly. But disposals use high volumes of water, at the sink and at the sewage treatment plant. Chunks of goo formerly known as dinner also increase sewage volume, requiring additional sewage-treatment capacity for municipalities already struggling with funding for existing plants.

Older, predisposal sewage systems may not have the right slope or capacity to handle wastewater with minestrone in it, leading to clogged pipes. Homes with septic tanks are well advised to avoid in-sink choppers, which will fill the tank quickly. To further complicate the issue, during the sewage-treatment process, large debris is removed to landfills.

Call your local sewage folks for more information, as these issues do vary by municipality. The answer will depend on the current configuration of sewer and solid waste problems in your area. But, as clean water comes at more and more of a premium, and as it gets harder to site and operate sewage treatment plants, the likely answer will be: Put noncompostable food scraps in the garbage.

AMERICAN IDLE

At last it's time to kick back and get down with your bad eco self. And you deserve to relax! Just try to do it with your eyes on the prize: a cleaner, greener, longer-lasting planet.

HIT THE BOTTLE

If you take the edge off of the day by knocking back a frosty beverage, spend a moment between swigs to consider the container. The can versus bottle dilemma is a tricky one, but a good basic rule is to drink locally bottled beer in glass bottles if you can.

As we discussed in our lunchtime chapter, manufacturing aluminum is resource-intensive. Virgin glass beverage containers are also made from an abundant natural material: sand, mixed with limestone. Extracting any resource removes part of the planet, shifting the environment for good or, more commonly, ill, and sand is no exception. But the transformation of sand into glass is easier and less energy intensive than the laborious journey from bauxite to aluminum. The finicky answer to the can-versus-bottle dilemma is that it depends how far

Those of you who feel a beer just isn't a beer unless it's paired with a zesty wedge of lime may be faced with a bit of a puzzle when it comes time to recycle your bottles. How do you get the lime out of the bottle, and if you can't, are you irreparably tainting the entire recycling system?

Two pseudo-scientifically tested methods for this quandary seem to meet with frequent success. One is sticking a chopstick down the neck and dragging out the lime, and the other is twisting the lime almost straight before inserting it. Please experiment at home and use your test results to reinvigorate happy hour chitchat.

But here's the answer to the larger question ("Mommy, where do beer bottles go?"). When you recycle your beer bottle, it's picked up by a hauling company, which brings it to a glass-cleaning plant, which then ships it to a glass-manufacturing plant, where it begins a new life. A "contaminant," as your lime would be called, is either picked out at pickup or removed during the cleaning. The only kinds of contaminants that are worrisome are those that, when melted down and incorporated into a new product, would somehow lower its quality—things like window glass, ceramic jars, or metal. If you were to somehow get a fork stuck in your beer bottle, it might disfigure and weaken future post-recycled bottles. But while too much organic debris can discolor new glass, your little lime won't do much damage.

In short, drink up, but don't forget to twist.

the packaging materials were shipped when raw, empty, and filled. The energy costs of producing aluminum would make glass clearly preferable, if glass weren't so darn heavy. Lightweight aluminum may have equal or better freight costs even if it is shipped farther. However, moving glass is expensive (environmentally and financially), so it's more likely to be kept in a regional waste stream. You see how easy it is to go insane in an attempt to do the right thing? Learning the travel history of a brew container is a lot to ask of the average drinker. If you have a decent local glass-recycling program, go with glass.

Drink to Your Health ...

It used to be that St. Patrick's Day was the only time you could swig green beer, but no longer. Lots of brewers are jumping on the organic bandwagon, from small fry like Fish Brewing Company (*www.fishbrewing.com*), Wolaver's (*www.wolavers.com*), Eel River (*www.eelriverbrewing.com*), and New Belgium (*www.newbelgium.com*) to the biggest beer bellies. Budweiser has quietly led its Clydesdales to drink with a new sub-brand called Green Valley Brewing, and Miller is distributing an organic brew too.

If you prefer the hard stuff, there's no shortage of organic options for your liquor cabinet, such as Square One vodka, Papagayo Organic rum, Highland Harvest whisky, and Juniper Green gin. At your next party, consider arranging an organic booze taste-test and see how the new stuff stands up to your old favorites. (And when your guests can't stand up themselves, order a round of cabs for everyone.)

In the perfect situation, your local brewer would be reusing bottles. Check around. But don't worry too much. Your beer can is just one of many uses for aluminum (and a rather small one, at that): Cars, buildings, airplanes, and more are all made with aluminum parts. And, of course, glass is also popular among the object-making businesses. So if you must worry, worry about the aluminum that went into your automobile, and make it last as long as you can.

FOR THOSE ABOUT TO ROCK

When you're in need of a musical interlude, are you more likely to pop a CD into the stereo or crank up your MP3 player? Are there best practices for ensuring your decibel diving isn't doing too much earthly damage? Music mavens take note.

A U.K. STUDY FOUND THAT PLASMA TVS USE FOUR TIMES THE ENERGY OF CATHODE-RAY MODELS.

CDs are made of clear polycarbonate backed with a reflective metal, usually aluminum. This involves injecting stuff into molds, which sounds fun and squirty, and as an added bonus, part of the process is called "sputtering." The disc is lacquered, the label silk-screened on, and the whole thing packaged in paper and plastic. The paper is usually virgin (nonre-cycled), and the plastic—well, unfortunately it's our old enemy, PVC.

The CD gets shipped (more environmental impact), we buy it, and we listen to it on a CD player or computer. These machines both contain the heavy metals customarily found in electronic devices. They also consume electricity.

When we tire of the CD, we sell it, donate it, or throw it away. If we are very good, we send it and its packaging to an "e-waste" recycler, like eRecycle (*www.erecycle.org*) or GreenDisk (*www.greendisk.com*). When the CD player itself goes to the great entertainment center in the sky, we probably discard it as well, since electronic-waste programs are still gaining steam. If we are very good, we check with groups like those mentioned above to find out where to take it instead.

An MP3 player is a small, computerized device, which, by necessity of purpose, fashion, and size, is also chock-a-block full of heavy metals. It uses (toxin-filled!) rechargeable batteries that may or may not eventually be recycled. To fill the player with music, you spend time downloading files—which, according to one study by Digital Europe, theoretically means 50% less resource consumption than buying CDs at a store or online. This is a substantial difference, but as the study points out, it can vary greatly depending on things like people's downloading habits and Internet connections.

When it comes to disposing of an MP3 player, we are also concerned about recycling. And there's the further complication of duration. You've had your CDs for 15 years. Will MP3 players find such permanence? Or will they be akin to cell phones, with each model quickly overthrown by the next generation? We suspect the latter, at least at this point in their development, which would mean more waste. The good news, in this case, is that Apple will take back old iPods, and Dell will take back any Dell-branded electronic product too.

This leaves us without an overly conclusive conclusion as to which music method is better. Of greater concern, however, is the fact that electronics manufacture and disposal is moving toward crisis proportions. Instead of worrying about how you play your music, worry about pressuring manufacturers and governments to require end-of-life take-back plans for electronic products. To get started, visit the EPA's product stewardship pages (*www.epa.gov/epr*), where you can learn more about state, federal, and international efforts to keep these toxics out of our landfills.

LET THE GAMES BEGIN

For some folks, the best way to unwind involves shooting imaginary weapons at imaginary people, monsters, and aliens. While this might counter some eco-ideals of peace and sustainability, video games do not inherently violate environmental principles. The main trouble is that they are played on computer equipment, which—as we've established—are fun machines filled with toxic substances.

The best idea is to purchase your computerized gizmos the way you should buy a car. First, test the gizmo and see if you even care for or "need" it. Then, gizmo-pool if you can—share with friends. You'll avoid the demand for toxic substances, and you'll be doing something vaguely social with an actual in-person person. (They can be pretty stimulating too!)

Your next active environmental moment is when obsolescence arrives in its dark cloak and scythe to claim the PlayStation. "Consumer electronics" cannot go to the dump because their components must be kept away from the general air and water supply. Some manufacturers will take back their machines. With most gaming hardware you'll need to find a decent general e-waste reclamation

If vids are your favorite pastime—or your kids' idea of a good time—check out these games with a green twist, available online or for your home system:

> Adventure Ecology (*www.adventureecology.com*): Interactive, online adventure sends players on missions against global warming.
> Food Force (*www.food-force.com*): Know who makes cool video games? The United Nations. For real! This one teaches kids about world hunger.
> Eco-Rangers: Animal Kingdom (*www.snaptvgames.com*): Good for younger kids, this DVD adventure takes players through a jungle of natural-world trivia.
> SimCity (*www.simcity.ea.com*): The classic civilization-building game brings urban planning and smart-growth issues into your living room.
> Greenpeace Games (*www.greenpeace.org/international/fun games/games*): Based on arcade classics, these offerings are earnest but entertaining (Nuclear Tetris, anyone?).
> Climate Challenge (*www.bbc.co.uk/sn/hottopics/ climatechange*): Good BBC brainteaser for anyone who wants to see what it's like to be a world leader in these troubled times.

site, or seek out a retro-gaming market that may be craving your old console. Unlike film and television production, game design does not use any materials except electricity and computing equipment—no elaborate sets or fake snow. And the discs, packaging, shipping, and advertising are about equal to DVDs and CDs. So the hardware is truly the big problem.

DIRTY MOVIES

Say your idea of a good night is a good flick. Can a green go to the movies with a clear conscience?

Right now Hollywood is facing an inconvenient truth: it's a dirty industry. A UCLA report says TV and film productions pollute more than four other local industries, including aerospace and semiconductor manufacturing (but likely less than oil refineries, so that's a comfort). Set construction, special effects, and other excesses emit 140,000 tons of ozone and particulate pollution a year, adding to L.A.'s notorious smog. While the report singles out a few films—including *The Day After Tomorrow*, which offset its carbon emissions, and two of *The Matrix* movies, which recycled 97% of their set materials—it says Tinseltown's "structure and culture hamper the pace of improvements." Reps for the industry, which employs 252,000 people in the L.A. area, were quick to defend their eco-cred, but not everyone is buying it. "They're not green at all except when they're forced to be," said Ted Reiff of ReUse People of America, which dismantled the *Matrix* sets. (He'll never work in that town again.)

Beyond the exorbitant environmental price of making movies, it's likely you'll drive to the theater to see the latest blockbuster (using gas), buy snacks for

In addition to today's techno-trash pile—CDs, DVDs, pagers, game cartridges, zip drives, jump drives, PDAs, MP3 players, digital cameras, cell phones, scanners and laptops—e-waste recycler GreenDisk can put your shameful past to good use. Visit the GreenDisk website to find out how to turn old embarrassments into shiny, shame-free products. May we make a few suggestions?

VHS Tapes

Whether it's your *Survivor* audition tape or the saucy show you produced for your partner that long-ago Valentine's Day, GreenDisk will take it with no questions asked (yes, even if it's Beta!). And never fear—your private moments won't end up on the Internet. GreenDisk uses a "degaussing" process that scrambles the magnetic registers on tape, assuring the erasure of delicate or personal materials.

Cassette Tapes

You know what we're talking about—that dust-covered pile of mixtapes from ages-old boyfriends? The labels are so faded you can't even read them anymore, which, come to think of it, is probably a very good thing. Time to say goodbye to "Summer Lovin'— '86 Rules!!!"

Laser Discs

Back in the day, you were very cutting edge ... for about five minutes.

munching (using energy and plastic), and use lots of napkins to wipe the extra butter from your hands. But there is one small, flickering light in the darkened theater: The Environmental Media Association (*www.ema-online.org*) serves as a bridge between Hollywood's entertainment industry and green organizations. The EMA holds an annual awards ceremony (complete with a green carpet!) that lauds films, TV shows, and companies that succeed in passing along ecologically sound messages and practices, and gives a "green seal" award for productions that make an effort to be more green behind the scenes.

A NEW LEAF

Do you count yourself among the few, the proud, who still read for pleasure? We (and our relieved publisher) salute you, and offer these eco-tomes—some classics, some newcomers—for your perusal.

› *Silent Spring* (1962), by Rachel Carson. The classic revelation about chemicals, modern living, and the priorities of the human race.

› *Cradle to Cradle: Remaking the Way We Make Things* (2002), by William McDonough and Michael Braungart. Two visionaries set a new course for industrial design.

› *Gaia* (1979), by James Lovelock. In which the Gaia hypothesis—the idea that Earth itself acts like a single organism—is laid out.

› *My Family and Other Animals* (1956), by Gerald Durrell. A naturalist's account of growing up in Corfu, Greece, in the 1940s.

- *Field Notes from a Catastrophe* (2006), by Elizabeth Kolbert. Accessible, engaging essays on the people behind the climate-change issue, from Alaska to the Netherlands.

- *A Sand County Almanac* (1949), by Aldo Leopold. Nature-writing classic mixes essay and editorial as it explores the personal and political sides of preservation.

- *Refuge: An Unnatural History of Family and Place* (1991), by Terry Tempest Williams. Personal tragedy and natural history weave together in this reflective work.

- *The Quest for Environmental Justice: Human Rights and the Politics of Pollution* (2005), edited by Robert Bullard. A look at the unequal environmental hazards faced by low-income and nonwhite communities.

- *Pilgrim at Tinker Creek* (1998), by Annie Dillard. How well do you know the place you call home? This contemplative essay collection looks beyond the surface.

- *Stark* (1993), by Ben Elton. A group of ultrarich people seek to save themselves while the planet collapses. It's "fiction"!

- *Heat: How to Stop the Planet from Burning* (2007), by George Monbiot. Think it's impossible to cut emissions and still have a swell life? Think again.

- *Grub: Ideas for an Urban Organic Kitchen* (2006), by Anna Lappé and Bryant Terry. Part history, part advice, part recipes, this guide will fill your head with delicious dreams.

- *Forty Signs of Rain* (2004), by Kim Stanley Robinson. First in a trilogy of near-future, D.C.-based novels by a prolific writer with other eco-trilogies to his name.

- *An Inconvenient Truth* (2006), by Al Gore. Need we say more?

Turning the Page

You don't have to be a fan of mysteries to figure this one out: Traditional book publishing uses massive amounts of virgin paper, chlorine, and toxic inks. With adult trade books gobbling up 500,000 tons of paper a year—or 8.5 million trees—some groups are encouraging the industry to scale back. Publishers including Random House, HarperCollins, and Scholastic have committed to using some paper certified as sustainable by the Forest Stewardship Council, and others (including ours! hooray!) are embracing recycled paper and soy inks. The news that the final installment of the *Harry Potter* series would be published on FSC-certified leaves offered a glimmer of hope that the industry was starting a new chapter.

LET'S GO TO BED

It's been a long, green day and at last it's time to hit the hay. (Don't worry—we are not about to recommend you use a mattress stuffed with lumpy straw.) Whether you use your bed for turning in or getting turned on, we have a few notes from the nightstand. And when it's time to turn off the lights forever, we offer some options for resting in peace.

WHAT'S IN YOUR LINEN CLOSET?

As you get ready to crawl into bed, take a moment to think about where you'll be sleeping. With any luck, you'll be breathing deeply for a long stretch—is the pillow supporting your noggin stuffed with organic wool or recycled rubber? What about those sheets you swaddle yourself in—are they made from hemp or organic cotton?

If you can't find eco-linens in mainstream stores, you can certainly find resources online. Bamboo linens are an unbelievably soft and eco-friendly choice, since bamboo is a rapidly renewable resource. In addition, bamboo sheets are inherently germ resistant, thanks to a naturally occurring property mysteriously referred to as "bamboo kun." Whatever kun is, it's both antifungal and antibacterial, and is the same reason bamboo crops never need pesticides. (No word on whether it keeps the bed bugs from biting.)

It's no dream: You can stock your linen closet with green fabrics. And if you do, how much easier it'll be to drift off to la-la-land. But if new sheets aren't in your future, at least wash the old ones in a natural detergent so you're not inhaling chemicals for eight hours.

Cuppa Tea?

If your soothing nighttime ritual involves a steaming cup of tea, you might reconsider the way you heat your cup of comfort. Quantity makes a difference when it comes to selecting the most efficient heating appliance, so if you crave just one serving of tea, the microwave is a better choice than heating the habitual pot of water on either an electric or gas stove. Or, if you are a truly dedicated range user, you could carefully pour one mug's worth of water into your kettle and heat only that. You'd be saving a tiny bit of energy, though it would be cancelled out by the energy you wasted on being niggly.

In addition, if you can bag the bags and switch your habit to loose tea, do. Tea companies began making tea bags so sippers wouldn't have to go to all the trouble of putting loose tea in a pot. Then they decided that individually wrapped tea bags connote a certain freshness, and pretty soon the shelves were jammed with double-bagged and -boxed tea, and the accompanying excessive packaging.

SAY NIGHT-NIGHT

The first step in your evening ritual may well be putting the kids to bed. As you shuffle your pajama-clad wee ones off to slumberland, keep these suggestions in mind to ensure you both have green dreams.

Beyond The Lorax

You've read it once, you've read it twice; wouldn't some other books be nice? Try these other eco-kid offerings on for size.

> *Farewell to Shady Glade*, Bill Peet
> Gaia Girls series, Lee Welles
> *The Gift of Nothing*, Patrick McDonnell
> *The Giving Tree*, Shel Silverstein
> *Tarka the Otter*, Henry Williamson
> *The Sea, the Storm, and the Mangrove Tangle*, Lynne Cherry
> *The Story of Ferdinand*, Munro Leaf
> *There Once Was a Sky Full of Stars*, Bob Crelin
> *Winnie the Pooh*, A. A. Milne

BATHTIME

> Choose bath toys that aren't made from vinyl (see sidebar).

> If you're sudsing up with bubble bath, avoid products with the ingredients "PEG," "polyethylene," "polyethylene glycol," "polyoxyethylene," "-eth-," or "-oxynol-." These chemicals come with a byproduct called 1,4-Dioxane, a suspected carcinogen that you probably don't want near your splashing spawn.

> Instead of conventional soap, use olive-oil–based or organic soap.

> Use that time to read or tell stories with a green bent.

> Dry them off with softer-than-soft bamboo towels.

BEDTIME

› Dress your kidlets in secondhand or organic cotton sleepwear—or one of your old T-shirts.

› Tuck sleepy youngsters into bed with organic, pesticide-free sheets and a wool mattress.

Rubber Ducky, You're Not the One

In December 2006, San Francisco became the first U.S. city to ban the manufacture, distribution, and sale of baby toys containing chemicals linked to cancer and developmental delays. The prime targets—bisphenol A and phthalates—have been found in everything from rubber duckies to teething rings to bathtime books. Concerned advocates say the chemicals can leach out when babies do that gnawing, gumming, sucking thing. "Protections for children from chemicals in toys are weak at best and dysfunctional at worst," says Joel Tickner, environmental health professor at the University of Massachusetts-Lowell. "Consumers would be astonished if they knew that federal laws regulating chemicals in children's toys all require balancing the benefits of protecting children with the costs to industry of implementing safer alternatives." Industry, kicking and screaming all the way, has sued to block enforcement of the EU-inspired ban, and city councillors are said to be reconsidering its scope.

> If they're prone to bedwetting, use a rubber or polypropylene mattress protector instead of one made from PVC.

> Read them *The Lorax* (1971), Dr. Seuss's delightful ode to conservation.

NAUGHTY BY NATURE

What if instead of winding down, you use bedtime for winding up? Let's consider the playthings you're using for grown-up fun between those organic sheets.

Few eco-conscious shoppers consider the chemicals used to create their intimate devices—from vibrators resembling long-eared bunny rabbits to sleeves and rings in shapes ranging from faux female to flower power. If these seem like unmentionables, that's part of the problem: while some are made with unsafe materials, it's tough to talk about it like, well, adults.

But it's necessary. Unlike other plastic items that humans put to biologically intimate use—like medical devices or chew-friendly children's toys—sex toys go largely unregulated and untested.

Many popular erotic toys are made of PVC and softened with phthalates, a controversial family of chemicals. These include invitingly soft "jelly" or "cyberskin" items, which have grown popular in the last decade or so, because the materials are cheap and easy to work with. The danger is that heat, agitation, and extended shelf life can accelerate the leaching of phthalates.

In recent years, testing has revealed the potentially serious health impacts of phthalates, including reproductive damage. So what's being done to protect consumers? Well, nothing. While parts of the United States, Japan, Canada, and the European Union have undertaken various restrictions regarding phthalates

Where You From, You Sexy Thing?

If customers select jelly playthings at Babeland, a retailer with stores in Los Angeles, New York City, and Seattle, the staff gives them a tip sheet on phthalates, and recommends using a condom with the toy.

Babeland staff also steer willing customers toward phthalate-free alternatives, such as hard plastic, or the silicone substitute VixSkin. Some manufacturers are also using thermoplastic elastomers instead of PVC. Vibratex recently reformulated the popular Rabbit Habit dual-action vibrator—made famous on *Sex and the City*—with this material. While alternative materials can be more expensive, when people have the option of choosing them, many do.

in children's toys, no such rules exist for adult toys. In order to be regulated in the United States under current law, sex toys would have to present what the federal government's Consumer Product Safety Commission calls a "substantial product hazard"—essentially, a danger from materials or design that, in the course of using the product as it's made to be used, could cause major injury or death. But if you look at the packaging of your average mock penis or ersatz

Norwegian Wood

There is no shortage of naked activists willing to carry on the legacy of Lady Godiva. But the award for Scandalous Naked Activists of the Year, if there were one, would have to go to the Norwegian nonprofit organization Fuck for Forest.

Founders Leona Johansson and Tommy Hol Ellingsen are a new breed of environmentalists—or perhaps a new breed of porn stars. With their paid-subscription website, they are raising cash to save the rainforest, one money shot at a time. And they're determined not to let their fellow environmentalists stand in their way.

Since Johansson and Ellingsen started the site with seed money from the Norwegian government, their effort has gained considerable notoriety in the European environmental community, winning both friends and enemies around the world—especially after an appearance at an outdoor music festival in Norway.

"How far are you willing to go to save the world?" Ellingsen asked from the stage—then proceeded to go all the way with his lady-love for about 10 minutes in front of an audience of several thousand.

The link between having public sex and saving the planet may seem tenuous at best. But consider this: According to a report by the U.S. National Research Council, the online porn industry rakes in between $5 billion and $7 billion per year. That's about as much as all U.S. environmental- and animal-welfare groups, combined, raised in 2004. Cashing in on the porn money machine could be a windfall for environmental groups—or so Ellingsen » believes. The music-festival stunt, despite gaining the pair a little legal trouble, appeared to be a net gain. In the three months after the couple's highly publicized arrest, the site attracted more than 1,000 new members—at $15 per member per month.

Whatever one may think of their morals, it's pretty savvy fundraising. But other green groups have been reluctant to, er, get in bed with the group, fearing that its brand of activism could tarnish their reputations. Ellingsen sees a certain irony in their reluctance, noting that we live in a world where public sex is considered far more controversial than wholesale ecological destruction. In fact, the group's website contains a warning on its entry page: "If you are underage or get offended by love or truth, you must exit this site now."

Despite the chilly reception the group got in Europe, it has found a loving embrace in warmer climes: Costa Rica and Ecuador. Partnering with local groups, it has helped with a reforestation project in the Amazon and helped protect more than 100 acres of rainforest elsewhere. It's a busy time, they say—after all, "liberating nature and sexuality is a big task."

vagina, it's probably been labeled as a "novelty," a gag gift not intended for actual use. That's an important semantic dodge that allows less scrupulous manufacturers to elude responsibility for potentially harmful materials, and to evade government regulation. If you stick it somewhere it wasn't meant to go, well—caveat emptor, baby!

So what are the other alternatives for eco-conscious pleasure-seekers? The most ecologically correct choices may be metal or hardened glass dildos—which, with their elegant, streamlined shapes (and sometimes hefty price tags) can double as modernist sculptures if you grow weary of their sensual charms.

And the eco-choices don't stop there. If you want to do your part for conservation while getting a buzz, go for the Solar Vibe, a bullet vibrator that comes wired to a small solar panel. (Talk about heating things up!)

Choosing the most eco-correct erotic toy can seem fraught with compromises—more akin to picking the most fuel-efficient automobile than buying a bunch of organic kale. With no government assessment or regulation on the immediate horizon, it's up to you, the consumer, to shop carefully and select a tool that's health-safe, fits your budget, and gets your rocks off. Meanwhile, pack up that old mystery-material toy and send it back to the manufacturer with a note that they can stick it where the sun don't shine.

STOP IN THE NAME OF LOVE

Like sex but fear the consequences? Let's talk about birth control.

In a perfect world, the most environmentally friendly birth control out of the available lineup would be the "natural" method, which for men translates to withdrawal (and an immaculate sense of timing), and for women means tracking fertility by charting daily temperatures. Certainly, this method has no manufacturing burdens, no waste, no packaging, no advertising, no electricity. But we're not perfect, and if the natural method fails—user error and unpredictable equipment can be a major problem with this one—you've got a potential environmental disaster on your hands: another North American.

Since the jury is still out on the repercussions of hormonal birth control methods ending up in our sewage systems, we'll move on to condoms. Generally made of latex, condoms are not recyclable (plus, used condoms would be revolting if gathered in bundles and shipped to a reclamation plant). Yes, this means they produce some waste, but in the grand scheme of things, this is one of those relatively inconsequential quandaries. In this case, the picture is even clearer: It is always more important to save your life, your reproductive system, and your brain from the havoc of an STD or the megasurprise of an unplanned child than it is to worry about a little piece of latex in the waste stream.

However! Never flush a condom: in addition to wasting water, they'll end up as sewage solids, and the sewage staff will have to pick them out and put them in the trash themselves. (More revolting.)

VEGAN CONDOMS? YOU BET. THEY'RE MADE WITH COCOA POWDER INSTEAD OF MILK PROTEIN.

COMPOST IN PEACE

While we're on the topic of sleep, we should raise the issue of eternal rest, or what we like to call the Great Green Beyond.

Lights Out

Is the bedside light you clap off each night an energy-efficient compact fluorescent?

If efficient, low-energy lighting were installed all around the world, global energy costs could be cut by nearly a tenth, says the International Energy Agency (IEA). The technology is widely available, would curb light pollution, and, according to a 2006 IEA report, could keep up to 16 billion tons of carbon out of the atmosphere over the next quarter century.

Today, artificial lighting accounts for nearly 20% of the world's electricity consumption, and "without rapid action, the amount of energy used for lighting will be 80% higher in 2030," says IEA Executive Director Claude Mandil. We're sure you can guess who could make the biggest impact: The average American home uses ten times the artificial light of the average Chinese home, and 30 times that of the average Indian home. The executive director of Greenpeace U.K. is urging governments to mandate efficient lighting in building codes, and Australia, the United Kingdom, and the United States have considered legislation that would phase out incandescent bulbs. What a bright idea!

There are more choices about the fate of your corpse than you might imagine. Let's start with the traditional options. Cremation is greener than burial, for (at least) three reasons:

1. Embalming (which is common although not mandatory) uses noxious chemicals to preserve the body.

2. The impenetrable bunkers that are the latest trend in caskets won't biodegrade anytime soon.

3. Cemeteries are usually high-maintenance parks full of pesticide-laden lawns kept trim by gasoline-powered mowers.

Cremation is not a wholly green process, since incineration does produce some air pollutants—but at least your ashes, unlike your casket-fortified body, can return to the earth.

Thanks to the modern death industry, however, we have plenty of more colorful options. If you seek to truly be a part of the earth, you could be cremated and have your ashes incorporated into artificial coral reefs. These large concrete blocks are being used to restore coastal fish habitat, and though your remains are not a vital part of the process, some companies (such as Eternal Reefs) offer you the option of becoming a postmortem part of ecological restoration. Your relations could scuba to your watery grave! Or, if you wish to be closer to your family, a better choice might be to have

yourself condensed into a low-carat artificial diamond. (Many diamonds, in fact: You are a carbon-based gem quarry, and, hey, turning yourself into bling doesn't require backbreaking low-paid labor from indigent people.)

But there's also an option designed specifically for earth conscious cadavers—the "green burial."

If you'd like your demise to contribute to a greener planet, reserve a plot at Forever Fernwood, a northern California cemetery specializing in "eco-interments." About half of Fernwood is devoted to burials that use environmentally friendly practices: hemp-silk blend shrouds, biodegradable coffins, low-key grave markers made from petrified wood, and no embalming. Fernwood owner Tyler Cassity is a wild child of the funeral world—he transformed a decrepit old Los Angeles-area cemetery into "Hollywood Forever," a destination location featuring weekend movie screenings on the side of Rudolph Valentino's mausoleum. While only a select few can hope to have their eternal resting place trampled by moviegoers with bags of popcorn, the green lean of millions of aging baby boomers is expected to create a very lucrative eco-burial market over the next few decades.

Of course the notoriously creepy "death care" industry, with its penchant for exorbitant coffins, high-falutin headstones, and all the trimmings, has a tendency to stiff-arm the green burial movement. Which is all the more reason that before you check out for good, you should check out the Green Burial Council (*www.greenburialcouncil.org*), which has developed a set of standards for green burials and provides information on the expanding list of green burial providers.

SLEEP ON IT

If you're staying up nights wondering what else you could be doing to help the planet, consider these extra-credit steps for overachieving greens.

› Write an environmental advice column for a neighborhood newsletter.

› Start a community garden in your neighborhood, or join one and get active.

› Start a neighborhood green group and take local action frequently, even if it is only on minor issues or small in scope.

› Offer to organize and sponsor chaperoned nature field trips for kids who otherwise might not be able to go on them.

› Volunteer your time to researchers who must regularly collect field data.

› Find out where farmers' markets are near your relatives, and send them directions and coupons.

› Convince your large employer to set up matching funds for donations to an environmental cause.

› Volunteer at your local arboretum, zoo, or aquarium.

› Challenge your friends and family to set and meet individual goals for cutting emissions (give eco-prizes! everyone loves a sink-side compost bin!).

› Fund-raise for solar panels in developing countries.

> Make sure everyone you know is supporting clean energy if it's available in your area.

> Let your local, state, and national representatives know you're watching, and their decisions on environmental issues matter to you.

Most of all, set an example—but in a nonpompous, nonpreachy way—by showing the people you love that living green doesn't mean changing who you are.

Evening Grist in Five Seconds or Less

The best environmental book I've read this year is:

A. *Silent Spring*
B. *Green Eggs and Ham*
C. *Anne of Green Gables*
D. This one, of course.

OK, we were looking for answer D, but to be honest, all of the above are great reads.... So go forth and greenify.

GOOD NIGHT, AND GOOD LUCK
YOUR TOP TEN QUESTIONS, ANSWERED

While the ultimate success of the sustainable movement will require a "don't miss the forest for the trees" perspective, most of us tend to get hung up in the branches—which is perfectly understandable. Accordingly, here are the top ten most frequently asked questions sent to Grist, so at the end of the day, you can have your answers once and for all.

Q. Should I use paper or plastic bags at the grocery store?

A. Neither one is better. Best choice: Bring your own cloth bag.

Q. Should I dry my hands with paper towels or the electric blow dryer?

A. Use the dryer if you can't drip dry.

Q. Should I wash my dishes by hand or use the dishwasher?

A. If you and your dishwasher are efficient, by all means bypass the sink.

Q. Is it better to leave (cars, lights, computers) on when I'm not using them, or turn them off and restart them?

A. Restart! Whether you're driving, defeating darkness, or doing work, it takes more energy to keep your power-suckers running than it does to turn them off and on.

Q. My old (car, refrigerator, washing machine) isn't energy efficient. Is it worse to keep using it, or to toss it and buy a new one?

A. In general, it's better to upgrade (whether washing machine, fridge, dishwasher, or car)—but make sure your old machine is reused or recycled if possible.

Q. Should I use cotton or disposable diapers?

A. We know you worry, parents, but honestly, it's a wash. Here's an idea: go diaperless!

Q. Which plastics are OK?

A. We don't like plastic, in general. But just make sure you avoid #3.

Q. Which is better: Diesel? Biodiesel? Straight vegetable oil? Hybrid?

A. They're all bad. Stop driving! But while you work toward that goal, see "Commute-icable Diseases" for a comparison of your options.

Q. Is it better to buy organic food from far away, or nonorganic food grown locally?

A. Ideally, buy food that is both organic and local—but if you have to choose, local is the way to go.

Q. I want to follow your recommendation and buy compact fluorescent lightbulbs, but I've discovered they contain mercury. What should I do?

A. Buy them anyway—the small amount of mercury (less than in a watch battery) can be handled by a hazardous-waste facility at the end of the bulbs' long life.

ACKNOWLEDGMENTS

First and foremost, this book would not be possible—and Grist would not be what it is—without the work of Umbra Fisk and Rebecca Warren, and without the vision of founder Chip Giller.

Thanks are also due to Brangien Davis, who managed to weave eight years of content into a logical narrative, to Heidi Smets, who made it look darn good on the page, to Kate Rogers at the Mountaineers Books, who conceived of the project with Grist's Kendra Howe and shepherded it with grace and flexibility, and to the rest of the Mountaineers team. And to Katharine Wroth, who shirked her other Grist duties to pitch in.

We're grateful to the community of writers who have contributed to Grist, including those whose work was mercilessly retooled herein. And, for providing invaluable feedback before and during the (vegan) sausage-making process, thanks to Grist staffers Trina Stout, Holly Richmond, Sarah Hardin, and Kate Sheppard.

We'd be remiss (and poor) if we didn't acknowledge those who have funded our nonprofit notions over the years, including most significantly the V. Kann Rasmussen Foundation and The Kendeda Fund. In addition, The Overbrook Foundation and the Weeden Foundation have provided key funding for our green-living coverage.

Finally, a big, sloppy kiss to our readers around the world for your devotion to us and to the planet. It wouldn't be any fun here without you.

Editor Brangien Davis would like to thank Maria Dolan, dear friend and personal guru for all things eco.

INDEX

grist

ENVIRONMENTAL NEWS
& COMMENTARY

www.grist.org

Got questions? Got ideas? Grist wants to hear 'em.

Visit **grist.org/wakeup** to spill your guts ...
Who knows? Maybe you'll inspire Volume 2!

With an audience of 750,000 and growing, Grist.org tells untold environmental stories, spotlights trends before they become trendy, and engages the apathetic—all with a dash of irreverence. Founded as an email newsletter by current president Chip Giller in 1999, the Seattle-based nonprofit has remained fiercely independent in its coverage. Grist has won numerous awards from both the environmental and online communities, and has been featured in *Vanity Fair*, *The New York Times*, *Newsweek*, *Outside*, and dozens of other national publications.

Brangien Davis is a writer and editor in Seattle and publisher of *Swivel* magazine, a literary journal.